YOU GOT ANYTHING STRONGER?

ALSO BY GABRIELLE UNION

WE'RE GOING TO NEED MORE WINE

YOU GOT ANYTHING STRONGER?

Stories

GABRIELLE UNION

WITH KEVIN CARR O'LEARY

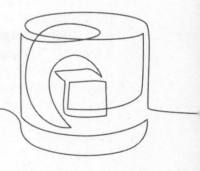

DEY ST.

An Imprint of WILLIAM MORROW

HarperCollins books may be purchased for educational, business, or sales promotional use. For information, please email the Special Markets Department at SPsales@harpercollins.com.

FIRST EDITION

Designed by Angela Boutin

Illustration © valenty/stock.adobe.com

Library of Congress Cataloging-in-Publication Data

Names: Union, Gabrielle, author.
Title: You got anything stronger? : stories / Gabrielle Union ;
    with Kevin Carr O'Leary.
Description: First edition. | New York, NY : Dey Street, [2021]
Identifiers: LCCN 2021020916 (print) | LCCN 2021020917 (ebook) |
    ISBN 9780062979933 (hardcover) | ISBN 9780063119710
    (hardcover) | ISBN 9780063214705 (hardcover) | ISBN
    9780062979940 (paperback) | ISBN 9780062979957 (ebook) |
    ISBN 9780062979964 | ISBN 9780063138674
Subjects: LCSH: Union, Gabrielle. | African American actresses—
    Biography. | Motion picture actors and actresses—Biography. |
    Television actors and actresses—Biography. | Infertility, Female—
    Patients—United States—Biography. | Motion picture industry—
    United States—Anecdotes. | LCGFT: Autobiographies. | Essays.
Classification: LCC PN2287.U55 A3 2021 (print) | LCC PN2287.U55
    (ebook) | DDC 791.4302/8092 [B]—dc23
LC record available at https://lccn.loc.gov/2021020916
LC ebook record available at https://lccn.loc.gov/2021020917

ISBN 978-0-06-297993-3

21 22 23 24 25 LSC 10 9 8 7 6 5 4 3 2 1

For Kaavia James and Zaya.

I am continually awed by the honor and responsibility
of raising free Black girls. May you each embrace
your vulnerability as your superpower, and may
I not falter as I attempt to lead by example.

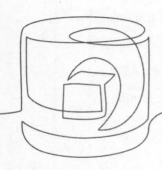

CONTENTS

INTRODUCTION

When I published my first book, *We're Going to Need More Wine,* in 2017, I opened by saying that it felt like you and I were on a first date. We each brought our expectations, not sure if this was going to go anywhere.

Well, we've progressed in our courtship. And this book is like us going away for that first weekend together. Because just as you think you know someone, it turns out you actually have no idea who a person really is until you've traveled with them. That's when you find out their bathroom habits, and if they're really the morning person they claimed to be on Instagram. And we also see how much baggage we bring along with us.

We are going on a journey, and for this, you're going to need something stronger.

I spent a long time planning this trip for you. Separately, we looked at the pictures of the house I picked for us to spend time in. "Oh my God, I can't wait for this trip to start," we said. And now we are here, and the house doesn't quite look like it did in the glossy pictures. The beach is farther than the host advertised, the Wi-Fi is wonky, and as we explore the house we find doors that are locked to us.

Still, we nervously assure each other, "It's charming."

And a few hours in, we realize it actually is. Sometimes the less bright and shiny a home looks, the more it offers. We can appreciate a house for its history—for what it has weathered, and how it's been lived in. See the places where someone has put love into it, the collaboration and collision of old and new construction. The house has great bones, it just needs tending to.

By the end of the first day, as if the house has warmed to us, we find the set of keys to those locked rooms. We are let in, trusted to see the photographs on the wall, the treasured books on shelves. All the signs of life and the good-ass energy that people were so purposeful in creating to fill this place. By the end of the journey, around when we really have a sense of the house and each other, this becomes our place.

As a lover of memoirs and biographies, I have benefited from authors revealing themselves so that, as readers, we can see *ourselves*. The truths collected in those pages—typed out letter by letter, as they were lived moment to moment—build a community of kindred strangers. I owe these writers a debt, and while I can never repay them, I can at least honor them by sharing my own truths here with you. Readers gather the courage to become storytellers, and the lifeline is passed, person to person, book by book. The message remains, *Keep going.*

There are people on the sidelines who will heckle us, lingering on the fringe just long enough to hear half a truth and twist even that into a weapon to run amuck with. I know from fellow readers who found kinship in my first book that efforts to shame me—in comments I probably never even saw—sent the message that it's too dangerous to be honest. Your story has no value, certainly not when you weigh it against the cost: the emotional toll of telling your truth, or the discomfort it *might* cause someone hearing it. Better to be silent, and remain alone.

You are not. We are here together in this moment, and we can have compassion for each other. But of course, that starts with giving it to ourselves. That is an ongoing project for me, one that I have had to continually start over and over again from scratch through the events of my life, collected here in this book. There's always something that lands you on your ass—even success, which comes with its own challenges. You think, *There's no way I can move on from this. I will never recover. I will never be the same.*

No, you won't be the same. Life, it turns out, is a series of mini deaths. And, thankfully, rebirths. You have to grieve the person you were before, and I have to acknowledge that I am not the same woman I was when I wrote to you four years ago. If you thought you knew me then, you are not alone. I thought I knew me, too.

So, let's raise a glass as we start our trip. Here's to getting to know each other better.

1

LOVED EVEN
AS A THOUGHT

So. Where were we?

Right, you and I left off in October 2017, when my first book came out. The weeks before the release were filled with dreams of loss. Pets dying. My husband leaving me. Babies not being born. My therapist told me those dreams were my soul preparing for my true self to emerge after letting go of my grief. In the book, I had finally spoken openly about my fertility journey. I was having second thoughts—in fact, so many thoughts they were organizing to go on strike. But I knew I had to stay honest because I didn't want other women going through IVF to feel as alone as I did. I had suffered in isolation, having so many miscarriages that I could not give an exact number. Strangers shared their own journeys and heartbreak with me. I had led with the truth, and it opened the door to compassion.

But from then on, it seemed every article about me used the phrase I had offered: "I have had eight or nine miscarriages." This was always followed closely by my age, which at that time was forty-four. At least that stopped reporters from asking the question I got at every red carpet: "When are you and Dwyane gonna have a baby?" But my openness about pregnancy loss led journalists, friends, and strangers at the supermarket to cock their heads and ask a new question. It was presented casually, but not offhand. No, this was a statement, disguised as a question, that people thought I needed to hear right now.

"Why don't you go the surrogacy route?"

Each time this was presented, I felt the constant, public prodding to acknowledge my body's failures. "Just let some other, more capable, woman get the job done. Because *you're* not capable." It wasn't my imagination. In life's many comment sections, it was clear that I had wasted enough of everyone's time. The messages were that I had prioritized my career, and now I was too old to have a kid. In fact, I owed that to Dwyane. I had robbed him of this child because I was an older woman—almost ten years older than D—and I had to have known my window was limited.

The reality is that I had been diagnosed with adenomyosis one year before, with the gag being that I'd had it since my early twenties. It was Dr. Kelly Baek, a freakishly intelligent, no-nonsense reproductive endocrinologist in L.A., who finally, accurately, diagnosed me with what every other doctor had missed. Before meeting her, I had gone through multiple rounds of IVF with leading doctors around the country. When you are in their offices you stare at the holiday cards behind them. Plump babies with beaming, relieved parents. Each baby is counted, with numbers reported to the CDC and officially tabulated to define that fertility clinic's "success rate." For the desperate like me, the CDC website has a handy table showing every clinic's numbers. Picking one just now at random, I see it says, "Pregnancies: 225," and then just below, "Deliveries: 177." Then that gets divvied down to patients using their own eggs, and those using donor eggs. Those success-rate numbers are everything to a doctor, and keeping them up is why doctors don't always want to work with older women or women with "unexplained infertility." When a clinic prefers winners only, there isn't much incentive to find an explanation. We, the worst cases, are simply weeded out.

But Dr. Baek saw the real issue at the first ultrasound, my uterus up there on a flat-screen in her exam room. "Oh," she said, "so, you have adenomyosis."

"What's that?"

She pointed at the screen, right at this little black spot in a black-and-white ocean. "You can see right here—it's endometriosis of the muscle." My endometrial tissue, which lines the uterus, had grown into the muscular wall of my uterus. She explained that as the fetus grows, the adenomyosis covers it like a blob. It was also responsible for my low ovarian reserve.

Dr. Baek asked what my periods had been like. I told her in my early twenties, I'd gotten used to them lasting for a third of the month, passing huge clots, and bleeding through overnight pads. Bleeding like I'd been shot in the vagina. Doctors had prescribed birth control to "regulate" my period, not mentioning birth control is great at contraception, but not so great at treating heavy periods. It causes the absence of a period. What many people mistake for their "regulated" period is just breakthrough bleeding from taking the placebo in the final week.

Then as soon as I wanted to start trying for a baby around 2013, I was advised to cut out the middleman—nature—and start IVF because of my age. At forty, I had come off the pill, then took a seat on a roller coaster of hormone injections. And then came the miscarriages. It would have been impossible for me to tell if my uncommonly long periods were just my body returning to whatever issue I had before I started using birth control.

Dr. Baek pointed to the ultrasound again. "So, I would say it started in your early twenties then. It's *pretty* pronounced, so I doubt this just arrived. I don't know how anyone would have missed this."

I looked at Dr. Baek. My world was suddenly slow motion. She crossed her arms. I looked at her pearl earrings, her hair tied back. I tried to focus on these details, but I was now adrift in that ocean on the screen, overcome all at once by waves of clarity, relief, and grief. Later, there would be anger that I had sat in the offices of the world's leading IVF doctors, and all they saw was my age. There was no investigation into any other cause for my miscarriages, and I was never correctly diagnosed or treated.

The first time we were pregnant, it was All-Star Weekend years before. We called everyone and told my stepchildren, Zaire, Dada, Dahveon, and Zaya. We shared our joy, and then it was snatched away. After me, I would say the kids took it the hardest. Zaire and Dada were preteens, and Zaya was seven. It was brutal, because in addition to loss we also had to explain the concept of miscarriage. They took it as death of a sibling they never met, and they had never experienced the death of anyone close to them. How were they to feel about the absence of someone they never knew?

After that, we stopped telling anyone when I was pregnant. Which was often. There were times this would happen "naturally," and times I would get pregnant with embryos implanted through

IVF. I isolated myself, wishing I didn't even have to involve Dwyane. Just deal with the shots and the positive pregnancy tests and the eventual spotting that signaled the beginning of another end. The reason I can't tell you how many miscarriages I have had is that my life became one long loss. I numbed myself, growing used to the fact that life was not a series of heartbreaks, but an unending feeling of failure and rejection.

I realized I was staring at Dr. Baek. I looked down. The worst thing about hope is that it remains to taunt you, just out of reach. I still tried everything. Not just IVF, but bargaining with God. What had I done that God decided I was just not worthy? Was this some karmic or cosmic retribution? I had consulted healers, one of whom had told me, "If we tap into your spiritual core, do a clearing, I bet we can get you to a place where you can conceive and carry." When all these measures failed—rituals, herbs, crystals, full moon chants—when I did all of the things you could possibly think of and none of them worked, maybe that just meant I was a bad person. And bad people were not worthy.

I returned my eyes to the ultrasound. The black dot.

"So, what do I do?" I could tell Dr. Baek was solutions-oriented.

"Your best chance for a healthy baby would be surrogacy."

I nodded. Silently.

I was not ready to do that. I wanted the experience of being pregnant. To watch my body expand and shift to accommodate this miracle inside me. Is that what it would be to experience true oneness with another being? I wanted my heart to be in sync with her—to beat for her, and then with her.

I also wanted the experience of being *publicly* pregnant. I envied how pregnant people were revered, immediately respected and trusted and loved upon, as a vessel of life. I would forever shake off the distrust society has for women who, for whatever reason—by choice or by nature—do not have babies. I had paid the cost of that for years, and I wanted something for it. I understood the logic that I had embryos ready to implant in a gestational carrier instead of me. There would be no genetic relation between our baby and the carrier; the genes would be solely Dwyane's and mine. But I still fought the idea.

I held out for a year after Dr. Baek suggested surrogacy, and instead chose to endure more IVF cycles and losses. Everyone comes to the decision differently. For me—for the person I was then, or was trying to be—choosing surrogacy would be acknowledging an "L." I was a batter, literally batting zero percent. Couldn't even get on base, and everyone in the outfield and all the positions was just pointing at me like, "*You . . .* you're just striking out. Enough already. Just bring in the pinch hitter."

The chant in my head began. "Pinch hitter! Pinch hitter!" It was my team saying it, then everyone in the stands, and even the guy in the parking lot selling throwbacks out of his trunk. Dr. Baek was now leading the chant, but D remained the loudest. He was excited at the prospect of our child. Finally, we could get on a route where we had a really good chance of ending up with a live birth. But I kept trying. With each subsequent loss, I heard, "We're losing the game, and bitch, you're getting older by the second. Give it up."

Near the end of that year—that hopeful and hopeless year—I had a new plan to take Lupron, which basically quiets the adenomyosis. The strategy was I would do it, then implant our embryo and hope it grew faster than the adenomyosis returned to cover it and snuff it out. I was told it would give me a 30 percent chance of bringing a baby to term. But the side effects of Lupron can be intense: you're basically throwing your body into early menopause and you can break bones very easily. Still, I was willing to take that risk for a 30 percent chance. Thirty sounds like a lot when you've had zero.

"Lemme go on with this and then circle back," I told Dwyane. *I would rather throw myself in front of home plate and get a hit-by-pitch*, I thought, *just so I can be awarded first base. Go down swinging before I call in this pinch hitter.*

D was quiet, then said, "You've done enough."

He said it with the authority of a coach doing the long slow walk to the pitcher's mound. I shot a look at him. There was a desperation just dripping off him that I couldn't ignore. A desperation of wanting things to be right with us. *His* journey was so different than mine. His was wrapped up in guilt and shame and embarrassment. And fear of losing me.

In 2013, before we were married, Dwyane had a baby with another woman. It should go without saying that we were not in a good place in our relationship at the time that child was conceived. But we were in a much better place when he finally told me about the pregnancy. To say I was devastated is to pick a word on a low shelf for convenience. There are people—strangers who I will never meet—who have been upset that I have not previously talked about that trauma. I have not had words, and even after untold amounts of therapy I am not sure I have them now. But truth matters.

"You've done enough," he said. I looked at D with an instantaneous white-hot rage. Astonishment, really. I was fighting with my husband about what was best for my body? Did he really think that surrogacy and a baby was our chance to set it right? To rebalance? I said coolly, "*You're* going to be the voice of reason *now*? Really? *Really?* Is that what we're on today?"

He looked me in the eye. "As much as we want this baby, I want you," he said slowly. "We've lost too much in our relationship for me to be okay with encouraging you to do one more thing to your body and your soul."

I read those words now and hear them again. I didn't receive this as concern at the time. It was an acknowledgment of failure. Because at that point I would have sold my soul for a win. To get out of the endless cycle of loss. What was the going rate for souls? What was mine worth, anyway? The experience of Dwyane having a baby so easily while I was unable to left my soul not just broken into pieces, but shattered into fine dust scattering in the wind. With desperate hands, we gathered what we could to slowly remake me into something new. There was no way to disguise where I'd been glued back together, so I was left to hope that the breakage and repair would at least be appreciated as history. A living contradiction of being solid but still broken; stronger and yet painfully delicate. But how do you value that soul?

The murmurs of the unseen crowd came at me again. "This woman is such a failure. *And* she has the nerve to be old. *And* she has the nerve to have a younger husband. *And* she has the nerve to stick with a guy who had a kid with somebody else."

Clearly, my feelings weren't originating from a healthy place. So much of what made the decision so difficult was that if I didn't submit to a surrogacy, then I was convinced I needed to let Dwyane go. Even if he didn't want to, I had to let him find someone who could give him what he wanted.

But I loved him. As our relationship went in and out through the years, the times when it wasn't even about romantic love, I always loved him. Each day, he had worked to be forgiven, and I had chosen to love him and forgive him. And part of this journey of making peace with our love is also making peace with ourselves. I had come to accept that without that awful collision in our lives—this Big Bang moment in our relationship that set our galaxy as we knew it—he wouldn't have become the man he desperately wanted to be, and I would not become the woman I dreamed of being. The astrophysics of love creates a dizzying paradox: The me of today would not have stayed with him, but would I be who I am now without that pain? That fiery explosion that created life and light? The advice I would give myself now would be to leave. "You don't have to do this. You don't think you have an option, but you do. Save yourself."

I remember a small voice in my heart saying just that. My fear of public humiliation was so great that I didn't take my own advice. In the aftermath, I invested so much time in making peace between us that I gave myself absolutely no self-care. And now there I was, still putting my life secondary to some shared mission. Why was I so willing to risk myself for a chance? If there was another way for me to bring my baby into the world, and have my health, why was it so hard for me to make peace with that?

Meanwhile, because I'd been public about my fertility issues, every interview eventually got to my miscarriages. One journalist asked me if I had learned anything about resilience from the experience. "I think I'm trying to learn the difference between resilience and neglecting my emotional reality," I said. "They can feel the same. One sounds empowering and one is not helpful at all. I haven't been able to figure that out consistently." What was me proving my strength, and what was me dismissing the glaring truth of my pain?

I chose not to do the Lupron and told Dr. Baek I wanted to use a gestational carrier. Finally, I had to walk away from home plate, dragging my bat behind me. Take a seat on the bench so I could watch everyone cheer for somebody else.

We had three healthy embryos left. "They're a hundred and ten years old," I told Dr. Baek. "My eggs are like the Dead Sea Scrolls. You'll have to bring in an archaeologist to certify their authenticity."

We chose the embryo to transfer, a girl. Now we needed someone to carry her.

———

For weeks, I went down a rabbit hole of books—both fiction and nonfiction—surrogacy message boards, and conversations with our fertility agency. I was struck that even in the ostensibly feel-good industry of having wanted babies, racism showed up. *You again?* I thought. *I know I can't escape you, but really? Even here?* Let me take you on the journey: At the top of the surrogate food chain were married white American women who have their own kids. The belief is that if they are married, they have a built-in support system, and if they have more than one child, there's proof they can do the job. There's extra credit if they have been a surrogate before. They know the ropes.

On the message boards, people can be anonymous, so they rank surrogates by race. I got the sense a lot of white families-to-be were more comfortable with brown people as surrogates—Latina and South Asian—who were often classified as "breeders." Now, I am Black, and I am used to hearing how people speak of women of color, but this was some *Handmaid's Tale* shit, and I stopped watching that after the first season. The pervading message was that if you were trying to be economical with the surrogacy journey, just find a womb housed in a brown body. They were literally lower-priced, and tended not to have the protections or fees of high-priced lawyers.

And the rate was indeed sliding. For a fee, there were people willing to let you dictate what the heck they eat, what shows they watch, what music they listen to, how much activity they do . . . So, I was this Black woman unable to have a child through my body, and here I was in this racial and ethical . . . does the word "quandary" even cover it?

We chose the most ethical agency we could find, and answered most of their questions about prerequisites with "We don't care." Religion, active lifestyle, diet . . . "Whatever you eat to have a healthy birth is fine with me," I said. Why would I, a failure, fix my mouth to give advice to someone who was clearly a pro?

"What about race?" they finally asked. "Is finding a Black surrogate important to you?"

"But it's the womb," I said. "If there's no genetic tie, what difference does it make?"

"*Welllll*, it matters to some people."

"Hunh," I said.

Here's the power of a book: As we were starting the interview process of finding a surrogate, I read *Little Fires Everywhere.* We were in Cleveland, where Dwyane was playing for the Cavaliers, and I went to the Barnes & Noble to buy that book the day it came out. It spoke to me because it has a surrogacy storyline and takes place in Shaker Heights, an affluent suburb of Cleveland. We had considered getting a place there, and I found that Shaker was all the things Celeste Ng talks about in her novel. That accuracy added credibility to how she presented the surrogacy experience. Skip to the next paragraph if you haven't read the book. A married couple asks one of the main characters, Mia, to artificially inseminate herself with the husband's sperm because she is such a look-alike of the wife, who is unable to carry a baby. Once she is pregnant, Mia reneges on the deal, takes off with the baby, and raises her child with no knowledge of her origins.

The book is so well written that it did not matter how much this scenario was unlike any surrogacy agreement we would enter. We'd have a gestational carrier carrying our embryo, and eventually a baby with no genetic tie to her. I bought right into the pop-culture story of the runaway surrogate. We felt that we could minimize that risk and fear by choosing a white surrogate. Because if she ran off with a Black-ass baby, people might be more inclined to ask questions. The fact that I was thinking about that shit tells you a lot about the emotional daze I was in.

Our agency began interviewing potential surrogates, and we got a hit in October with a woman who had multiple kids and had been a surrogate before. The agency does background checks, not just on the potential surrogates, but their spouses and anybody who would have any interaction with her as a pregnant person. *Oh, that's deep,* I thought. And kind of Big Brother–ish. As a Black person who is so surveilled in America, that threw me. Could I ask someone to submit to passing a test I wasn't sure my own extended family would survive?

In the vetting process, this person didn't disclose that her brother-in-law had been arrested for something. Someone from our agency acted personally offended, and though I was not, I did find it ironic that white surrogates had been prioritized and she was the one who lied about having a family member in trouble with the law. The agency was adamant that I move on. "We can no longer trust her," I was informed. So, it was back to the drawing board.

Two months later, in early December, we were presented with a surrogate who seemed to check all the boxes. We were introduced over the phone, but the conversation I had with her and her husband was made awkward by the fact that we couldn't reveal our identities to initially protect the anonymity of both parties. She said all the right things about how she had experienced the gift of life having her own kids, and wanted to give this gift to others. But I was cautious, having done so much research that I wondered if people were prepped to say that. Nobody's going to say, "I need this money, so take my uterus." That's not going to feel good for anybody.

After she was cleared by Dr. Baek, who did her own interview and medical workup, we agreed to meet in person in her office. As I got dressed that morning, I realized this was like the best and worst blind date ever. I wondered what outfit said, "I'm grateful, but I'm also not a loser. I'm an actress, but I'm not Hollywood. I'm not some Hollywood actress, you know, farming out her responsibilities." I wish I could tell you what I chose, but it's been blocked out by that oppressive fear of being judged. I was not comfortable in what I saw as my failure, but I also did not want to fail at this, too. Because this woman and her husband had the power to look at me and say, "Ennh . . ." I desperately needed this person to like me and accept me. Accept *us,* since I was standing in also for Dwyane, who was in the middle of the season. I was very aware that the surrogate and her husband didn't know we were Black.

I got there early because I am psychotic and early for everything. Dr. Baek put me in a small office, and the liaison from our agency arrived. "Are you okay?" she asked. "Are you comfortable?"

I smiled and nodded, unable to put words to the feelings. There had been so much fear and failure, but now there was a vague relief that I was finally here. And something else: anticipation. I had not let myself have that for so long that I had difficulty recognizing it.

The door opened.

Like a blind date, you look everywhere at once, knowing you are being looked at, too. The first thing I noticed was a nose ring. *Oh,* I thought, *she's a* cool-ass *white girl.*

And then I noticed her notice me. Her eyebrows shot up. "Oh, ho ho ho," she said. There was an excitement to her voice and I smiled. "This is such a trip. I have your book on hold at four different libraries."

And I knew (a) she was a reader and (b) she frequented libraries. I have never been done wrong by readers. I started laughing, and we hugged.

"So, I guess now I can get a copy, huh?" she joked.

"Yeah," I said, meaning yes to everything. Her name was Natalie, and when her husband came in I saw they matched. Earthy free spirits with an aura of goodness to them. They had an easy rapport and were openly affectionate with each other. I hadn't known that would be so important to me, knowing that she had a partner in this. I called D and put him on speaker, and as they directed their attention to the phone, I looked up at them. I don't know if I would have trusted everyone's explanation for why they wanted to be a surrogate. It might even be more comfortable for some people if it was clear that this was done for financial reasons. But these guys were legit. *You're those people,* I thought. *You really want to help others.*

I was very aware that we only had three embryos. If I was going to trust one of those prized embryos to someone, I felt like I could trust a reader.

"She has a nose ring," I told Dwyane when I called from the car after. "I don't know why that makes her even more trustworthy . . ."

"This is good," he said.

"Yeah," I said, scrunching my eyes into a wince. "Yeah."

———

We were back in Dr. Baek's office in February, this time in an exam room for the embryo transfer. Natalie lay on the table, knees up with a sheet covering her, and her husband and me on either side of her. I went alone, because Dwyane was still playing.

The room was darkened to better show the ultrasound Dr. Baek used to guide the catheter into Natalie's uterus for the transfer of this tiny embryo. The embryo that would become our daughter. The lower light added to the feeling that this was something sacred, and on-screen, we were able to watch the catheter go into Natalie's uterus as Dr. Baek narrated everything we were seeing. When I am nervous, I usually crack jokes to put myself and other people at ease. But I was quiet.

The moment she pressed the plunger to transfer the embryo there was this bright burst of light into the void. It was like watching the birth of a star. I gasped, unable to help myself, and Natalie smiled. We knew we would have to wait two weeks for a pregnancy test, but for now we all kept our eyes on this starburst. We just had to hope that the light stayed bright and was not extinguished. As it had been so many times in my body.

As we waited those two weeks, there was a sense of angels surrounding Dwyane and me, and now this baby. His longtime agent Hank Thomas had died in January, and he was more of a father figure to Dwyane than an agent. It was at his funeral that D mended fences with Pat Riley, the Miami Heat's team president and his former coach. It felt like a righting of wrongs and a new beginning. And it signaled his return to the Heat on February 9, 2018. Five days later, seventeen-year-old Joaquin Oliver was shot and killed outside his creative writing class at Marjory Stoneman Douglas High School in Parkland, Florida. He was among the fourteen students and three staff members murdered that Valentine's Day. Joaquin was such a huge fan of D's that his parents knew he would want to be buried in his #3 Heat jersey. D had always been conscious of his impact outside basketball, but in that time, I watched him become clear about his responsibility as a leader in society, in culture, and in our family. At the first home game after the shooting, Dwyane wrote Joaquin's name on his sneakers and hit an impossible game-winner in a 102–101 victory. He scored fifteen of the final seventeen points, and the feeling in the arena was that Joaquin was there.

In this surreal four-week span, Dwyane and I had seen death and created life. When we got the positive pregnancy test, my first thought was "Wow. Shit. This is really happening." The due date was Thanksgiving. A little too on the nose, but there it was.

In the midst of this, I had started filming the pilot for *L.A.'s Finest,* a series I would star in and executive produce. I'd built the production around the idea that with proper planning and communication, a boss can prioritize parenting for employees and employers, and still run everything efficiently. When I'd asked Jessica Alba to be my costar, she didn't think it was possible.

"I just gave birth," she had said. "I'm nursing."

"I got you," I assured her. "This makes you the best person for the job. You're somebody who best knows how to use time. If we run a great production, you will have all the time in the world to nurse." I believed that if we planned it right, we could change the mentality surrounding working mothers and active parents in the industry. Just by welcoming breastfeeding in the workplace and bringing kids to the office, we could signal a slight change in perspective to show people that nourishing a child is not a nuisance. Communicating and planning—the things we don't do well in Hollywood—were what we needed to attract people who actually wanted to get home for bedtime and feed their kids.

From that first pilot, it worked. We created what we had never seen, and I could see it in the way Jessica was able to do her work and parent with the help of our crew. I didn't tell anyone that I created a world for her that I was hoping to have for myself. Natalie was still only in the beginning of her first trimester, but things were going well. I pictured taking my daughter to the set and having a crib in my trailer. If it took a pinch hitter to have that dream, hell, I'd cheer her on, too.

We'd even begun to pick out names. When I was in my twenties and thought my life was going to be a little different, I'd begun keeping lists of baby names. There was one name I saw at the end credits of a TV show or movie: Tavia. *Well, that would be pretty,* I thought, *with a K. Kavia.* That name made it onto every new, hopeful list I kept.

Dwyane knew the list by heart, too, and we both felt it. This hope, this starburst, was her.

I was in a production meeting for *L.A.'s Finest* when Dr. Baek called. I stepped out of the room as soon as I saw her number. With remarkable care and directness, she told me Natalie was spotting.

"Oh," I said. This was always the first sign I was miscarrying. "Oh," I said again, meaning, "Fuck, come on. No. Come *on.*"

There was an issue with her cervix. Dr. Baek said Natalie would have to go on bed rest right away.

"So, it's not a miscarriage," I said, adding a quiet "yet."

"No," she said, with kindness in her voice. "But there is a fifty-fifty chance that she will miscarry."

All the joy, the *euphoria,* that I had felt watching my starburst of a daughter be shot into the womb . . . I let it go. Within seconds, after years of loss, my mind knew just how to keep this at arm's length. If I connected to this baby, she would be taken from me at any moment. I cursed myself for getting comfortable. And in those seconds, there was another thought: my baby was rejecting somebody else for once. My embryos didn't just find *me* unworthy, they even refused to thrive in this perfect, proven winner. Even the pinch hitter struggled. It wasn't just me.

I had to deliver this news to Dwyane, after being the bearer of this kind of news so many times. Oh, God, here comes the fucking Grim Reaper again? I was always crushed first by my own realization, and then again seeing that pain and disappointment in his face. Now, Dwyane had so much going on that he was not emotionally fragile, but open. He'd lost his father figure, and was handling all of the love, and also the responsibility, that came upon our return to Miami. *And* he was playing incredible basketball. In the midst of this wildly heartbreaking and high-stakes time in his life, I was very aware that the positive pregnancy test—knowing our daughter was coming—was something he held on to with everything he had.

And now I had to take it away. I hit his number. "She's spotting," I said. He knew exactly what that meant. "It's fifty-fifty. She needs to go on bed rest."

"Fifty-fifty," he said.

I left my body, floating over myself. And I stayed there. I watched Dwyane and Natalie, and her husband, become very present in how they approached this moment. Natalie went on bed rest, and I knew what an added hardship that was on her and her family. A stranger had committed to this, knowing this was a possibility in theory. But life happens. Life is the doing.

D prayed. It was near the end of the season, and Dwyane began to secretly write our daughter's name on his sneakers for games, the same way he had done to honor Joaquin. No one knew what it meant. She was with him, no matter the space or risk between them.

Me? I continued to float just above the scene, very aware that I was a balloon that could drift away at any moment. In exploring the dark parts of myself, I understand my version of dissociative fugue, a disappearing act I do under stress that can involve literal fleeing or, in this case, an emotional departure from my surroundings and circumstances. I fought it, trying to get back into this experience. I needed to tie myself to someone's wrist, but I was not ready to tether myself to this embryo. My attachment could only bring harm.

The closest I could get was Natalie. I reached down from the air to fasten myself to her with a loose knot. I started conversations about books we'd read, sharing experiences I could still keep at a slight distance. Things that were safe.

Over the passage of weeks and books, the bed rest seemed to be working. The embryo's heartbeat remained strong, and the issue with Natalie's cervix mended itself. Near the end of the first trimester, we all returned to Dr. Baek's office, this time with Dwyane, for the first 4-D ultrasound. Two couples crowded into a room built for one, awkward in our affection for each other, yet still feeling like strangers. This was the first time Dwyane had even met Natalie and her husband in person, and our hugs were those of people who did not know each other but had survived something as a unit. She was showing me her stomach, turning to the side, cupping the weight of my own maternal ineptitude. This growing bump that everyone thought I wanted to see was now a visual manifestation of my failure. I smiled, wanting to show I—we—were so happy and grateful. Absolutely there was that genuine feeling. But part of me felt more worthless. My pinch hitter was knocking it out of the park. I couldn't hit a ball and not only was she hitting every curveball, but when they changed pitchers in the middle of the count, she was still hitting 'em. A regular Babe Ruth, calling her shot.

And I was the statistician, taking notes on weight and BPMs. It's like Ring Night, when you're looking at the twelfth guy on the championship team like, "Are you really gonna wear that ring? You didn't do shit. You didn't even play."

Natalie lay down for Dr. Baek to pass the ultrasound wand over the bump. "There she is," she said.

And she was. There. Here. This very clear little baby in there. Her big-ass head, her spine, her little heart pumping, pumping, pumping. Determined to live. It was suddenly incredibly real. Dwyane took my hand, and there was so much happiness on his face, I lost it. My cry was a choke stopped up in my throat, tears streaming down.

It was grief. I'd had nine miscarriages. I say the following with the caveat that I am steadfast in being pro-choice. I was on a fertility journey at forty-four. The smallest cell was weighted with the expectation of life. A zygote was a baby, just on potential alone. When one of my eggs was examined, that was a baby. When Dwyane got a sperm analysis, that was a baby. Every swimmer was *our* baby. But when I miscarried in the first trimester, I never thought I had lost a *baby* baby. I had never let it count. Looking at the screen, I understood how many potential babies I had lost. That's why I was crying. A floodgate of grief and sorrow overcame me, threatened to drown me.

I saw my husband so happy, and I was not a part of it. I felt a chasm widening between us. I was embarrassed to be crying so much, but everyone was looking at me with smiles and nods. They thought these were tears of gratitude. The awe of witnessing the start of life. *I* was reliving death. Of course I was grateful, it would be impossible not to be. But what I was grateful for was that *this* life might be spared. That that heartbeat might continue, beat strong for decades, long after my own stopped. So many had stopped inside me. "Nope, I'm making it," this heartbeat said. "It was just you, bitch. Just you."

I allowed the misreading of my tears. Crying conveyed my gratitude and showed that I was a good mom. My first performance in
competitive mothering. Nailed it.

We told the kids soon after, at the beginning of the second trimester. We wanted them to feel part of the surrogacy journey, but
made them pledge not to tell anyone. We'd had a celebrity friend
whose surrogate was hunted by photographers. We didn't want that
for Natalie.

"And anything can happen," I added.

I said it quickly, as an aside. A shadow fell on their faces, swift,
like a cloud blocking out the sun for just a second. They already
knew that.

———

I was on the other side of the world from my daughter when I began
to let myself look forward to her arrival. We were in Beijing on business for Dwyane, who is insanely popular in China. We brought
friends with us. It was the end of July, the five-month mark we
had never made it to. Dwyane's sureness was something to behold
and envy. He was so certain she was going to make it that we told
our friends. After my first miscarriage, I had never ever told people
when we were expecting. Even this felt dangerous. The words were
out of my mouth to my friends and I thought, *What the fuck did I
just do?*

Dwyane broke out whiskey and cigars, and he announced that
he wanted to get a tattoo of her name on his shoulders. By then
we had added a second "a" to her name—Kaavia—because we
were convinced people would pronounce her name with the long
a of "cave" if we kept it with one. There was something about her
that told me she needed two names, so we called her Kaavia James,

after my uncle and godfather, James Glass. My uncle is one of the freest spirits I have known. Funny, intelligent, and unapologetically Black.

Dwyane wanted to get the tattoo that night, her name on both shoulders, written where his Heat jersey would cover it. I was terrified of the permanency. As he sat before me with his shirt off, I placed my hands where her name would be, and kissed the top of his head. I thought of something he would sometimes say to himself and to others: "My belief is stronger than your doubt." He usually said this when he was counted out after an injury, or walking away from a deal everyone thought he was crazy to turn away. But this was different. I didn't know if his belief was strong enough for both of us.

It would have to be. My fear continued to make me dissociate from reality. When we came home to L.A., I devoured every parenting podcast, book, and blog. I am someone who overprepares for everything. I rehearse ordering a pizza. All of it stuck, but I couldn't imagine putting it into practice. I was studying for a test I never thought I would be able to take.

I realized I was ready to parent well, but not to mother. I'd made sure Kaavia James got the very best womb with a hip surrogacy family who played the Earth, Wind & Fire, Hall & Oates, and Luther Vandross I requested. But I kept her at arm's length, because she could still be snatched away. She didn't feel part of me, the emotional thing that a lot of women have told me they felt while they were carrying. That grounding connection that I physically did not have, and that I wasn't allowing myself to have emotionally.

I wanted to talk about it with my mom, but I was never that daughter. I had been parented well, and I was mothered well, but I rejected much of that. I felt a natural allergy to being "smother-mothered," as I call it, and needed my independence. Growing up,

I was always clear with my mom that I was not the kid who needed to be rocked to sleep. I didn't want the huggy, hovery kind of mom, and my mom had always seemed to understand that mothering is not one-size-fits-all. My two sisters and my three adoptive young siblings—two teens and a preteen who my mom adopted at birth as a single-parent senior—all needed different things.

And yet, when I have been at my darkest, when I wanted to be comforted or soothed, I heard a mantra. *I want my mom. I just want my mom. I want my mom.* That's what I said in my head, but I never called on her. Not once.

When I called to tell her about Kaavia James, I surprised myself by asking for her. "Mom, she's due at Thanksgiving," I said, trying to sound casual but landing on awkward. "Are you cool to be able to, you know, come in for that . . . ?" I trailed off. I didn't want her to be there, like, *holding* me. I just needed to know that she was there supporting me in this next thing in my life. And frankly, I think I was still holding on to this idea of what childbirth is supposed to look like. A woman is supposed to have her husband and her mother there.

"Oh yeah, yeah," she said quickly. "I'll find someone to watch the kids. I'll be there, no problem."

If she was surprised, she didn't let on. When I hung up, I wondered if she'd always been ready to be there, waiting my whole life while I kept her just out of reach. Motherhood as a standing army. Not always active duty, but ready when called.

I decided to tell my dad when we flew out for the Nebraska Cornhuskers home opener. Before that, we told my uncle James outside a bar the night before the game. He was so happy for us. "We wanted to name her after somebody that means the world to me," I said. "So, our daughter, Kaavia James—"

"Oh, wow," he said, overcome. Dwyane pulled the collar of his shirt aside to show the new tats of her name. "Oh, wow," he said again, starting to cry. I'd never seen my uncle cry. He was the guy who saw sadness and switched up the music, poured a drink, and knew how to make everyone forget their troubles. Through tears, in so many words, he told me he knew how much we wanted this miracle child, and was touched that I thought so highly of him that we wanted to honor him this way.

I was excited to tell my dad and wanted it to be part of a huge night we had planned. We'd flown him out from Arizona for the game, his first home opener. His first Cornhusker game, period. My dad was seventy-four, born and raised in Nebraska as the biggest Cornhusker fan, but had never been to a game. The thing is that pretty much everyone in Nebraska—every ethnicity—is a massive Cornhusker fan, but when you physically go to the game, other than the Black people on the field, there aren't many others in the stadium watching the games. A lot of people have willed their tickets to the next generation, so the crowd remains white.

So, this night would be extra special. I planned on telling him at Memorial Stadium after the game. Or maybe during, I wasn't sure. Whenever the moment felt perfect. We got there early, and noticed the skies were threatening as we spent about thirty minutes taking pictures with fans. Dwyane was in a Cornhuskers jersey the university gave him, custom-made with his number. He was in a euphoric mood, taking selfies with anyone who asked. My dad was beaming, turning his head around to take in being so close to the field. I loved being on the edge of knowing I was about to tell him this wonderful news.

But ten minutes into the game, lightning flashed over Lincoln, and they announced a rain delay. We went to the airport hangar to

24

wait out the rain. I was so nervous, pacing around, that we finally decided to just tell him.

"So, Dad," I said, "we are expecting our daughter on Thanksgiving via surrogate."

He looked at me, holding out his hand like he was deciphering a riddle. "No shit?" he said. And then he looked at my stomach. I realized the riddle was how I wasn't showing if I was pregnant with a baby due in two months. As he stared at my stomach, it was this immediate kick to the teeth.

"Oh, nooooo," I said. "She's being born by a *surrogate*." On the one hand, I was getting to tell my dad that he is finally going to have this grandchild that he has wanted from me, and asked about nonstop, since my late twenties. But I had to explain that no, *I* am not able to physically give you this child, but she's coming. It felt like explaining failure during a win.

"Are ya gonna let her see her kid after?" he asked.

Her kid. I had to explain surrogacy to him, and no matter what, the concept wasn't getting through that this baby was genetically mine and Dwyane's. And also, I wanted to be mindful that every fertility journey is different. This baby would be no less mine if she came to us through an egg donation or sperm donation, or adoption.

He joked about me having to find someone to get the job done, and it stung. It still stings now. My father communicates through sarcasm and digs, and for years that was my default with people I loved, too. We matched wits with put-downs, but it's something *I'm* consciously working on not doing, and I've changed. Now, it doesn't feel like my dad and me bonding, it feels like the opposite. There was no denying he was excited, while at the same time remaining so defiantly confused about how surrogacy works that I wondered if he was doing a bit. But, now my parents both knew.

As I began to tell more friends, they were literally overjoyed, their happiness spilling over to a point that I sometimes physically stepped back. As they tried to show how beside themselves they were with anticipation, I nodded and smiled. They all asked when I would be having a baby shower.

"Let's wait until she's here," I'd say, looking down. I'd tempted fate enough.

The *L.A.'s Finest* pilot had been picked up, so I had to tell my employer, executive producer Jerry Bruckheimer, and Sony, our production studio. You know, "Hey, don't tell anyone, but I'm having a baby via surrogate. She's coming on Thanksgiving." I fantasized that they would be completely thrown and it would cause all these issues. Nope, they were thrilled. Then I remembered that I was the boss, as well. I had created the workplace of a parent's dream for Jessica. I just still couldn't fathom it being mine, too.

They started talking about quietly outfitting my trailer to make it baby-friendly, basically preparing for the birth of the golden child. A celebrity mom I knew suggested a baby nurse, and was alarmed that I had not lined one up already. My complete and utter lack of physical preparation was apparent when the nurse started in-person meetings to get to know us and prep our new house in L.A., which we were still in the process of moving into. I saw the alarm on her face as she realized nothing was ready. Finally, she just said, "Where's the baby gonna *go*? And where am I gonna sleep?"

"Oh, it'll be fine," I said, bluffing. "It'll be finished."

Nothing had changed by the next meeting. Imagine *A Baby Story* meets *Flip or Flop* with the HGTV narrator tut-tutting, "Gab said she wanted a baby for years, but now, at crunch time, the nursery's not complete. They don't even have window treatments."

Things finally started to fall into place as we headed into October, inching closer to her Thanksgiving due date. My trailer was ready, and all the things were ready at home. A beautiful nursery and a closet that rivaled a starlet's. Picture-perfect preparation on paper, with everyone ready except Kaav's mother.

I could busy myself throughout the day, but there was no blocking out the thought at night. Brushing my teeth the night before my birthday in late October, I looked at myself in the mirror. *You're gonna be a whole-ass forty-five,* I thought, *and teen moms are more prepared than you are.*

———

A week after my birthday, I was on my way to the gym before work. It was 11 A.M., and I'd been on the set late the night before. I had what I call my wig braids in, the prison cornrows I put my hair in so I can just pop my work wig on when I get there.

My phone rang. I looked down and saw Natalie's name. Natalie, her husband, Dwyane, and I were all in a group text chain, and that's how we usually talked unless we arranged a call. I pressed the speaker.

"My water broke," she said.

"Hunh?" I said.

I know, I know. I try to pay so much attention to words and my response was "Hunh?" I had Kaavia James's due date in my mind as set. She would be here at Thanksgiving. I was just getting used to it being November.

"I'm headed to the hospital now," she said.

"Okay!" I said. "Okay."

I called D. He was in Miami, and in the first few weeks of his final NBA season, which the media had christened "One Last Dance" as soon as he announced his retirement two months prior.

"Natalie's water broke."

"I can get there by eight P.M.," he said. He'd had a plane on standby for just this moment. He called the pilot right away.

"Just get here as fast as you can," I said, having no clue how fast these things go. "Hopefully you get here in time."

I called my mom. She picked up quick, like there was a call sheet that went out that morning that didn't include me. "I'll get on the first flight."

I realized I was still driving to the gym. Some magical thinking took hold, and I wondered if I should still work out before work. *Shit, work,* I thought. I called them, and they had a whole plan and would put it into motion. Of course they had a plan—we were that kind of set. Friend o' Mothers. They would shoot all of Jessica's stuff, which meant she was going to have to work every day to compensate while I was out on maternity leave.

I called Jessica. "No problem," she said, going into Robomom mode. "On it."

The car was silent when I hung up. "Uh, well," I said to myself. "That was fast." So right, D and my mom were on their way, I didn't have to worry about work . . . the baby nurse. I had to call the baby nurse. Again, *she* picked up right away. Unbeknownst to me, she was hunkering down in town in case the baby came early. "Thank God," I said, "because that had just not occurred to me."

By then at least I realized I wasn't going to the gym. I turned around to head home and get the bag I'd packed. Of course, I had the perfect bag packed—I wanted that A-plus. I had done all the things I was supposed to do, but this wasn't how I pictured it. I looked in the mirror quick, and saw my prison braids. I called my friend and hairstylist Larry Sims.

"I've gotta drive down to the hospital," I said. "But I, um, uhh, look crazy. And I know I'm gonna take pictures and I don't want to look crazy. Can you, um, come and put a wig on me?" I laughed. He came right over. Off I went.

On the way down, a friend texted me that a tabloid TV show was working on a story that I had moved out on D and was living on my own in California while he and the rest of the family were in Miami. We were splitting up. It was over.

"Oh," I said, laughing to myself. She didn't know about Kaavia James at all. I thought of a dozen or so replies, then hit her back: "We're good."

We reserved a hotel and rushed to our surrogate, descending on this hospital in no time. My mom got there before Dwyane. She is a reader like me—favoring Black mystery and sci-fi by authors like Walter Mosley and Octavia Butler—and she'd brought so many books with her that I realized she wasn't sure if I wanted her physically in the room. She was prepared to bide her time if her arm's-length daughter would have her sit in a hallway somewhere. D arrived in his black Sweet Sixteen hoodie, commemorating his sixteenth season in the NBA, and the baby nurse and her crew were there with these very Republican-looking Ann Coulter Collection receiving gowns steamed and hanging in the hospital room.

And then our surrogate proceeded to go into labor for thirty-eight hours.

At first, it seemed like this was just the home stretch. We'd waited this long, right? But it went on so long that Kaavia James was in danger. There was some hemming and hawing about doing a C-section, but then the doctor had to do an emergency one because the umbilical cord had become tied around Kaav's ankle. Now that I am Kaavia James's mother, I know that she tied it herself because she was simply over it.

Dwyane and I gowned up in white scrubs with white masks and blue bonnets to take seats in the OR. "It's time," said Dwyane.

I definitely didn't know how C-sections work. Turns out it's all kinds of rough. But it was fast, and suddenly the doctor was just holding her up for us to our wide-eyed gaze. Our baby sat in the doctor's left palm with her head supported by the right hand.

"Oh my God," I said. The room was festive almost, people saying over and over, "Congratulations." Just as quick, the doctor placed her on a little exam table and asked, "Do you have a name, you guys?"

"Kaavia," I said, my voice a choke.

"Hunh?" she asked, not hearing.

I put my hand to my throat to stop it from seizing up. "Kaavia," I said again.

"Kaavia," everyone repeated in joy.

This baby, given a name written on a wish list for decades, then tattooed on her father's shoulders. Given a name to summon her into existence—into being. She was loved even as an idea. Her very essence was loved and nurtured and supported even as a *thought*.

My body seized in a full release of every emotion. Relief, anxiety, terror, joy, resentment, disbelief, gratitude . . . and also, disconnection. I had hoped that the second I saw her, there would be a moment of locking in. I looked over at Natalie and her husband. There was a stillness to them. I had tied my balloon self to Natalie's wrist. *Wait, it's over,* I thought. *Wait.* I looked at Kaavia James on the table, and then back at them. It took all of us to create her, so I wanted us to share this time with them.

As Natalie went to the recovery room, Kaav was taken to the newborn nursery. Dwyane, my mom, and I all reassembled in a hospital room, waiting for them to weigh Kaav and clean her up. I put on a surgical gown for modesty so I could do skin-to-skin bonding with her. My mother and D were crying, our surrogate was crying, our baby nurses were crying, and I was a mess. We put on a mix, a playlist that Dwyane's agent and father figure Hank had made us before he died. He used to make us playlists for every occasion, and we wanted him to be there with us in this moment. The room filled with the opening bass riff of Bill Withers's "Lovely Day." He sings about being troubled, beaten down, hopeless. "Then I look at you," he sings. "And the world's all right with me." Just as he hit that line, the door opened and Kaavia James was brought into our lives.

Dwyane and I moved to a hospital bed, the same one we'd shared waiting for her arrival. My mother put a blanket over me and I pulled my gown down to hold Kaav to my chest.

"She has D's mouth, and her nose looks just like D's," I said. I love my husband, so to see his beauty reflected in our child was a gift. My mother kissed my cheek, and put her arm around me.

Kaavia James opened her eyes to look at me. She already had this freakish neck strength, more than any infant I had seen.

"It's us," I said, excitement in my voice. "It's us. It's your people."

"It's your people!" Dwyane repeated.

My mom held her, and we were all so emotional in this perfect moment. She returned Kaav to my arms, and I sat up to hold her as my mom slipped into the bathroom. I had wondered what it would feel like, this bonding time. Would it kick in then? My main thought was, *What is happening? They're not going to let me leave here with this whole-ass baby, are they?*

My mom came out, and I noticed she had a hand to the wall. "I just—" And she fell. Simply collapsed, and if D had not been standing right there to catch her, she would have hit the ground hard.

She was drenched in sweat, and looked like she was having a heart attack. The nurse happened to come in just as she fell, and called for help. Within seconds, they were taking my mom away.

I was in shock. She was around the same age as my grandmother when she died of complications from diabetes, which my mom also has. In fact, I realized she was around the age of all my grandparents when they died.

I couldn't speak, except to keep repeating, "Oh, God." *This can't be how the story is written,* I thought. If I wrote this, critics would be like, "Ennh, it's a little on the nose. The miracle baby arrives and they finally have this full-circle, three-generation moment, *annnnd . . .* she dies."

I went from euphoria to terror. Holding my daughter, I started thinking about all the things I wished I had shared with my mom. All the questions I wanted to ask. If this was the last moment with my mother, could I be confident that she knew me? Who I am, in my soul? She did such a great job of raising an independent young woman that not only did I never need to rely on a man, I didn't need to rely on my parents. What opportunities of connection had I squandered? How can I know my daughter if I never let my mom know me?

I was so grateful I'd had the impulse months before to want my mom there.

"She got on the first flight," I said. She was there for me.

Dwyane looked down at his phone. He was obviously missing that night's game in Miami, and the team announced he was out for "personal reasons." It was the first game he'd missed in his final season, and anytime an athlete says "personal" it opens them up to a thousand more questions. Who's dead? Is it a drug problem? Your problem or hers? Is it one of the kids?

There was an AP bulletin about him calling out, but there was always a press corps following him everywhere. Speculation started to go wild. People had paid a lot of money for what might be their last chance to see D. Wade play. And he was *missing?!*

I was thinking about how this would juice up that tabloid report about us splitting when a doctor came in. My mom hadn't had a heart attack, it was her diabetes. Her numbers were so out of whack that she'd gotten overheated and passed out. They were bringing her levels back to a safe zone and would monitor her until the next day. So, Kaav and my mother spent the night in the hospital, while we worked on sneaking D out to the hotel without being seen. We didn't want it to look like he was on some sort of weird vacation, or have the news of Kaav's birth get out before we had a chance to get her safely home.

A little bit after I got back to the hotel, my sixteen-year-old step-son Zaire texted me. "I'm so excited for you," he wrote. "You deserve this. To raise one of us from scratch."

"You deserve this." Zaire knew enough that he had to assure me I deserved this. As adults, we think we can shield kids from things. From conversations, from experiences, from reality. After that first loss, I thought I was protecting him and the other kids by not sharing with them. But they were witnesses. They knew.

In that moment, I saw *them* see all the red needle receptacles in the house when I was doing IVF. Red, with a skull and crossbones. All the different nurses who came to our different homes. All the hushed conversations and arguments we assumed they didn't hear. The physical changes in my body, the attitude shifts. The energy shift that fell on the house after every loss. They may not have known specifics, but they felt the need, and the loss. And most of all, the feeling of brokenness. I didn't articulate out loud that I felt that

I was unworthy of a body that would not betray me, but they felt it and shared in it.

I didn't want them to be part of my heartbreak, and the whole time they were experiencing their own. They were left to deal with those feelings alone. Now, even faced with whatever Zaire might be feeling about his place in the family—in my heart and D's—with whatever shifts this new baby might bring, he still wanted me to know I was deserving of motherhood.

But was I? At discharge the next day, they handed me Kaavia James. They told me she had jaundice, which yellowed her skin. They were very casual about it, sending us home with a UV blanket. "Put her in a window and turn her like a rotisserie chicken and she'll be fine," I was told. "Good luck." Oh, and here's your mom, too. Try to be a better daughter.

As soon as we got back to the house, we made the announcement about Kaav, and also that D would be taking two weeks' paternity leave. He did this partly in a show of solidarity with me, but also because he wanted to bond with Kaav. The mentality about professional athletes is "get right back in and play the sport," and that's if they even take off for the birth. But our journey was different. She had to learn both our heartbeats now.

We posted three photos of when we three met, sitting on the bed in that hospital room, along with the lyrics to Bill Withers's "Lovely Day." I said that she arrived the night before via surrogate. I got a lot of congratulations, and I got a lot of hate.

"Why does she have a gown on? She's acting like she had the baby."

"That's what Hollywood people do. They pay someone to have your kid."

"I thought this was her child?"

There were meaner ones, and they're all still up. People with laugh-crying emojis accusing me of hiding my inability to, as one put it, "breed." It fed into my feeling of not being worthy. You are a fraud, I was told over and over again. You are not who you say you are.

And I took it from there, damning myself for feeling over-whelmed by providing basic care for my child. *And you damn near killed your mama*, I thought. My mom, by the way, who had to go home to take care of her three other kids.

When she left, I felt all eyes on me in the house. I could tell my husband wanted to see me mothering our child. This had been his dream for so long. Visitors kept stepping back to get a wide angle on this mothering I had talked about wanting to do. The funny thing about an open-concept house is that there aren't many places to be alone. There were so many people around that I was never once alone with Kaavia James, and then became afraid to because she seemed so fragile. It felt, moment to moment, like the stakes were life and death. Even when I had the intellectual knowledge, it wasn't a natural instinct that kicked in. What was natural was a sense of responsibility. I could give you the A to Z of childcare, but was it instinctual? Hell, no.

For Dwyane, it was second nature. He's been an involved parent half his life. When he had Zaire at age twenty, he was an athlete on scholarship. He and his ex-wife were on WIC and had to share parenting duties to survive, so there was no day care. School, prac-tice, home. This was reliving that experience with resources. I found myself jealous that he'd been Teen Mom. And anything he did with Kaav was celebrated by onlookers—nannies, family members, and strangers alike—as if it were Fourth of July fireworks and Christmas morning presents all in one.

"How lucky you are," someone said to me when Dwyane went to expertly change a diaper. When I held my baby, there was always someone around to comment. "Careful, hold her neck up." Of course I did, as you would any baby, even one with Kaavia James's neck strength from birth. But when I'd place my hand on her head to lock her in, Kaav would still fuss and cry. I felt awful, like I was doing it all wrong.

Dwyane went back to work after the two weeks, and I struggled. It felt like I was on a set, about to do a scene with Viola Davis. And the director says, "Okay, now let the tears fall and say the lines." And my mind was a blank. The biggest job I've waited on my whole life, and as we get to take 110, we're running out of film and I've lost the patience and confidence of the crew.

I was in the nursery with Kaavia James and a baby nurse one afternoon. We were getting ready to feed her when the nurse stepped out to get something. I sat in the chair, holding Kaav, when I realized that this was the very first time we had been alone. There had always been someone around.

"Hi," I said.

Just then, Kaav, with her amazing neck strength, lifted her head from my chest and locked her eyes on mine. As much as she resembled my husband, the look she gave me was that of a mini-me.

"Girl, please," the look said. "You know what? Stop stressing. I'mma give them nothing but unbothered side-eye. And I'mma take the pressure off you. Cause I'm a whole-ass character myself. Don't worry. I got you."

I felt it in my heart. I don't pretend it was maternal instinct finally kicking in. It was my daughter telling me who I was by being who she is. Did I think I was number one on the call sheet? Kaavia James turned me into a character actress in her one-woman show.

The nurse came back, and I took a cloth from her. "We're good," I said. "Thank you."

We settled in, just Kaavia James and me. Instead of me trying to be something for Kaav or anyone else, I let her tell me who she was. I listened to her, even before she had words. When she had fussed about me worrying over her neck, I now knew she was saying, "If you don't get your hand from the back of my head . . . I don't need you to do all that *for me*. I'm not like other babies."

She was like me. My mother knew I was independent from birth, because she must have had a moment like this where she listened to me. Yes, Kaav needed care and parenting like any tiny human, just like I had. But we valued our independence, and the best mothering for that is to value it, too. If I chose to fuss over her, it was because I wanted to, not because I had to perform motherhood. She was not interested in *that* mom.

"I got you," I said, holding her.

———

So much time has passed. So many firsts. Yet the question lingers in my mind: I will always wonder if Kaav would love me more if I had carried her. Would she kiss me quicker or hug me longer? Would our bond be even tighter? I will never know what it would have been like to carry this rock star inside me. To see my body change to accommodate her greatness as I felt her make a home within me.

When they say having a child is like having your heart outside your body, that's all I know. Kaavia James was never *in* my body. I could not nourish her, and she could not find safety there. We met as strangers, the sound of my voice and my heartbeat foreign to her. It's a pain that has dimmed but remains present in my fears that I was not, and never will be, enough.

And Dwyane leaves me with another riddle that has no answer. I can never know if my failure to carry a child put a ceiling on the love my husband has for me. Yes, I am Baby Mama number three, a label that is supposed to be an insult. But is the injury really the asterisk next to my name in the record? The asterisk denotes that the achievement is in question. "She didn't really earn the title."

If I am telling the fullness of our stories, of our three lives together, I must tell the truths I live with. I have learned that you can be honest and loving at the same time.

I'm writing this poolside, because to be with my daughter is to be at least water-adjacent. Kaav's loved it from the beginning. Dwyane is in there with her, along with Zaire and Dada. No one is hovering over her in her water wings—they stay just close enough for her to feel the sureness of them. Zaya is sitting by me, taking it all in.

We're listening to Kaav's favorite, Luther Vandross. "Never Too Much" just came on, and Luther asks if the object of his adoration remembers a time when he was scared to show his love, fearing that he wouldn't be worthy of love returned.

"You must have known that I had feelings deep enough to swim in / That's when you opened up your heart and told me to come in."

I catch Kaav's eye, and she smiles back at me. And with that, dear reader, I have to get in the pool now.

2

DREAM TEAM

I saw a ghost last night.

Dwyane and I were on the couch, halfway through the latest episode of *The Last Dance,* the Michael Jordan docuseries on ESPN. Five episodes in, the show had become my Sunday night obsession. As a lifelong sports fan, it was my heaven.

Kaavia James had other plans, however, and grabbed the remote. She somehow managed to push every button at once, and the screen blacked out.

"Kaav," I said, as she turned to try to climb onto the couch, unbothered. She was the show, as usual.

When I got the television working again, Jordan appeared on-screen at the 1992 Summer Olympics in Barcelona, walking with

Magic Johnson in their USA jerseys. Together, they were the official and unofficial leaders of the Dream Team, the greatest collection of basketball talent ever assembled.

At first sight of those jerseys, I had a vague feeling of being pulled back into something. I tried to ignore it, and turned to Dwyane. I talked, too loudly for our living room. "Of course you chose number nine, too," I said. He'd picked Jordan's Team USA number when he played in the 2008 Olympics in Beijing. Dwyane smiled, but the feeling didn't leave me. I put my hand out for Kaav. To ground me.

As the episode went on and the Dream Team's performance at the 1992 Olympics played out, I had an increasing feeling of—not quite déjà vu, but of being drawn into a room in the depth of my being. Like the beginning of an old movie, where the dust is blown off books, and sheets are pulled off furniture to reveal the life that once was there. The room in my mind became more familiar, and beneath one final shroud, there was a ghost.

It was me, a broken nineteen-year-old curled up on my parents' couch that summer of 1992 in Pleasanton, California. I had been raped, and was so mentally destroyed that my only tether to the world outside our living room was the round-the-clock coverage of the Olympics.

I have told the story of my rape before, and have purposely done so since the beginning of my career. Rape is the most underreported crime worldwide, and it can also be the most isolating crime for a victim to endure. People needed to see someone they recognized who could still manage to function in the world, even pursue dreams. Besides doing interviews, I have spent years lobbying Congress and state legislatures about the treatment of people who have been raped. After doing this work for twenty-five years, speaking about my experience to shed light on what others go through, I am able to quickly and dispassionately rattle off the three pertinent facts of my case: In 1992, I was raped at gunpoint and severely beaten by a man robbing the Payless shoe store where I worked the summer before my sophomore year of college. I had the luxury of being raped by a stranger in an affluent neighborhood, so no one questioned my story and I received excellent care, which is not the case for the majority of Black survivors of rape. Once I was at school, I sought the help of the Rape Crisis Center at UCLA, and through the program's group therapy I began to see a path from rape victim to survivor.

And yet, people forget. There is the "Wait, what?" every time I talk about being raped. I sometimes wonder if it's because we have decided what a person who has been raped looks like, and part of me feels a second of relief that I don't appear to be a victim. At least of *that*. And another part of me wants to say, "Yes, I was the victim of a gun-toting rapist, and you know what else? I fought him. I grabbed his gun and fired off one shot on some superhero shit. I missed and was beaten more for it, but hey, I got a shot in." But no, I don't even get the mythology of that. No superhero origin story for me.

Seeing Jordan and Magic in their Olympic jerseys, however, I remembered what I had erased from memory. This teenager, devastated in every way you could think of, physically and spiritually, looking for heroes on a TV screen. I had two black eyes and my face was so bruised it was green and blue, so swollen I saw the Elephant Man in the mirror the one time I let myself look. My rapist was still out there—somewhere, and in my mind, everywhere. The last I'd seen of him was his back, casually walking out the fire exit of the storeroom where I'd pleaded for my life.

Those weeks after the rape are not the story I tell. I skip ahead. Yes, I have talked about the death of who I was before, and the person who rose up from the ashes. But what made up those ashes?

The truth is, what I had lost was the cloak of respectability that my parents trained me to think would protect me.

They had moved us to the predominantly white community of Pleasanton, California. Growing up there, the thing I heard from my white classmates was "You're different than other Black people." I made them feel better about their racism and notion of white supremacy. If I shape-shifted constantly to make white people comfortable by being the appropriate, reasonable, *good* Black person, I would get something in return. Their trust, access to opportunities, and safety.

I knew that part of my father's heartbreak about my rape was that he and my mother had worked hard to price themselves out of such things. I believed in that, too. We were in this perfect planned community, and I in turn behaved perfectly. I was an athlete who got good grades, dressed appropriately, and spoke the Queen's English. That cloak of respectability lay heavy over me, and it both defined and confined my identity as I grew up beneath it. But I would be safe.

While I was being raped, I left my body and looked down at that girl. *This doesn't happen to good people,* I thought. When that illusion was taken from me, I was left completely exposed, literally stripped and violated.

My "recovery" began at home, mostly alone. My boyfriend had seen me at the hospital, and his devastation was such that once I was home, I didn't want to tell anyone but my closest friends. My parents and older sister worked full-time at telecommunications jobs and had to carry on with life. My little sister was in and out, mostly out. Only *my* life had stopped. As a family, we'd started a routine that would define all of our interactions. I did not want to be seen, so it was best to pretend not to see me, and they would also get used to me disappearing because of my PTSD.

"Where's Nickie?" one would ask.

"*Oh,* she's literally crouched behind a door, hiding," I can hear them say, quiet, as if the person should know better. "Act like you don't see it. It's fine. Gotta go . . ."

It became impolite to ask what I was doing.

I was nineteen. The body wants to live, even if we don't know how. Red blood cells rush to the cut, and some chemical signal tells them to produce collagen to create new tissue at the wound. New skin begins to form, and the edges of the cut pull to reach each other until the wound closes to leave a scar. I felt a visceral need to heal and to be whole, though I didn't know how to will that into action. A different version of me had to start somewhere, and it began by watching the Olympics.

In the Before, the person who I was had looked forward to the Olympics for weeks. She was an athlete, someone who loved to watch gymnastics, track and field, and basketball especially, but there was always some random sport to get interested in. Four years before, she had very strong feelings about the redemptive arc of the South Korean team getting the gold in women's handball.

Now, I watched the opening ceremony with eyes that were nearly swollen shut, no longer crying because even the Kleenex touching my face hurt. There he was, hard to miss even if the cameras weren't focused on him: Magic Johnson in the athlete parade, six foot nine in his Team USA–issued blue blazer. There had been so much conversation about who would be on the Dream Team—the first time professional athletes would compete—and so much of it focused on whether or not it was safe for Magic to play. That previous November, he had learned he was HIV-positive during a routine physical. He'd retired immediately, at just thirty-two. HIV was so stigmatized in 1992—and still is—but back then to such a degree that

Australia threatened to boycott rather than play against Magic, on the grounds that just to be close to him would be to risk infection. Would the guys on the team even accept him?

In the parade, I watched Magic and that mile-long electric smile of his, Scottie Pippen beaming next to him. People said Magic was finished when he retired, and here he was smiling. Again and again, the announcer returned to comment on Magic as athletes from all over the world broke away from their own teams just to be near him. To pat his shoulder, to hug his waist. They were doing everything they could to be close to someone who had been deemed untouchable.

I felt a single, solitary pulse in my heart. Not a leap, or anything anyone else but me could register, but a sign of life.

———

The next day, Sunday, the phone rang and rang. One of my longtime friends had gone to a party and told everyone what happened to me, adding details with her imagination when facts were missing. The story was repeated and repeated. With every telling, the bashing of my face with the butt of a gun grew more severe, the images of my trauma more horrible. One constant in every retelling was that it was a Black man who raped me. All of these white people, who had allowed me to walk among them, now gasped that I'd been so damaged "by one of her own people." People wondered if I'd known him and asked what I was wearing that had invited this to happen.

I had walked among them, so smug in my assimilation that maybe they thought I deserved to be taken down a peg. Reminded who I was.

I let the phone ring and focused on the Olympics instead. That Sunday the USA basketball team took on Angola in their opener.

Olympic broadcasters were already following every move of the Dream Team, focusing on the stars: Jordan, Magic, Pippen, Charles Barkley, David Robinson, Patrick Ewing . . . Each was a Black lead in his own storyline, and though NBC packaged each as compelling in the Olympic tradition, they didn't need to. Each man transcended any production-team vision to own his story of excellence. Unapologetic in their Blackness and stardom, these superstars did nothing to dispel the notion that they thought they were too good and too rich to stay in the Olympic Village. Anyone who questioned this got their answer when any of the players hit Las Ramblas in Barcelona. They were mobbed like gods, worshipped by growing throngs of people literally looking up at their bemused faces. As Americans, they were bringing dominance back to basketball in the Olympics, restoring order with Black excellence, not even three months after L.A. burned in the protests over four officers' being acquitted of using excessive force in the arrest of Rodney King. On camera, which was novel then, the cops had struck the twenty-five-year-old with batons at least fifty times, burned his chest with a stun gun, and broke both his right ankle and a facial bone.

After the acquittal, the prosecuting team proposed a theory: maybe the defense's playing the videotape over and over again, so often in slow motion, had caused the jurors to simply become "desensitized." There was no longer any stirring of a collective conscience. This is the norm today, when we see autoplay tweets of Black individuals and families murdered, assaulted, and disrespected on a trauma loop we cannot escape.

I would propose that to worry people are desensitized is to assume the jurors, and most people, were ever sensitive to Black pain to begin with.

Like now, the U.S. was anything but a good place to be Black in 1992, but these larger-than-life Avengers were representing our country. Was this rebranding of America on a global scale problematic? Was white patriarchy trying to show that it loved Black people by lifting up these men? None of that occurred to me at the time. I needed a lifeline, and what I saw was unapologetic Black stardom and perseverance.

The next evening, July 27, my boyfriend came over with his brother. I had always been so embarrassed by our living room, and now I felt trapped there. It was cheap, econo-luxe without the luxe. The couch had a hole in it for years, one my parents covered with a throw that always had to stay in place.

At the hospital, my boyfriend had nearly collapsed in tears at the first sight of me. He kept repeating my name, sadder and quieter each time, like he was chained to something that was falling away deeper and deeper into darkness. Me. I couldn't fully grasp what caused his grief. What percentage of his desolation was that this had happened to me, and how much was it that this had happened to *his* girlfriend?

I kept the TV on while he sat on a chair far away from the couch. His brother, an assistant college basketball coach, stood awkwardly in the room until he finally sat. I stared at the screen, and out of the corner of a swollen eye, I could see the brother's face turning back and forth from the TV to my face. He was here as an ambassador for my boyfriend's family, who were Greek and Mexican. They were cordial to my face, but my boyfriend made no secret that they called him a nigger lover when I wasn't around. They had always begged him to dump me, but the brother was here to back up what my boyfriend had to say that day: now that his family saw how heartbroken he was over my rape, they understood this love was real.

It was like they'd come from a faraway shore to greet me on my desolate island. To bring me the good news that I now mattered. In the face of my trauma, his reaction was what the family needed to see me as human.

I still wouldn't look at them. A Gatorade commercial was on, blasting in the room. People running around in the bright sun in the world going on outside the living room. I didn't know what his brother wanted. Gratitude that my plight stirred something in their consciences? A nigger lover, yes, but *this* nigger was somehow different.

The U.S.-Croatia basketball game came on and I was relieved they focused their attention on the screen. This was a big one, with Croatia being the one team that could stand out against the U.S. My boyfriend's brother talked about the Croatia forward, Toni Kukoč, getting drafted by Chicago, as if I didn't already know. The general manager, Jerry Krause, was obsessed with Kukoč. This white player from Croatia was going to be the future of the Bulls. The current and future kings of the Bulls, Jordan and Pippen, disagreed. The announcers kept talking about Jordan and Pippen shutting Kukoč out, only letting him get four points the entire game. "Oh, man," my boyfriend's brother kept saying.

"They're incredible," I said softly.

It must have been the first thing I said the whole game, because they looked over at me quickly and the speed of it made me flinch. I resented the sign of weakness, and I had a flicker of anger. *What made my boyfriend's family worthy of defining* my *worthiness?* I asked myself, not ready to ask this out loud.

Meanwhile, over in Livermore, a fifteen-minute drive from where we sat in the rubble of my life, my rapist was about to strike again. He had been in and out of the Clothestime store at the Pepper Tree Shopping Center during the day, and then, as he had done at my

Payless, he returned just at closing. It was slightly before nine o'clock at night, and he got in saying he wanted to buy something for his girlfriend. Once in, he pulled a gun on the two women working there, a nineteen-year-old and a twenty-year-old. Like me, he had them walk in front of him at gunpoint to the backroom, where he ordered them to undress. He raped the nineteen-year-old girl, and sexually assaulted the twenty-year-old.

The girl he raped convinced him that if they weren't all out of there by thirty minutes after closing time, an alarm would be triggered and police would come.

My rapist, now our rapist, fled into the July night.

Eight miles away, I exhaled when my boyfriend and his brother let themselves out. Eventually, I waited long enough that I thought I might trick myself into falling asleep in my bedroom. I brushed my teeth without looking in the mirror I had studied myself in for years.

In bed with the lights on, I again smelled the gunpowder from the shot I'd gotten off and missed. I did not close my eyes.

———

Days later, a manhunt was on. The rapist was photographed at another Payless, and police tied him to a fourteen-day spree of robberies and rapes. He turned out to be a former Payless employee, which explained his understanding of our closing schedule. They staked out his mother's home and after a few days, he turned himself in. My father told me his name, and I was struck by the fact that it was just a slightly different spelling of a Nebraska Cornhuskers football player I had cheered for. *What a terrible, weird coincidence,* I thought. It's my only tie to my rapist's name. From that moment on, if I heard that name, I thought only of the football player. My rapist's name was and will always be Rapist. According to a court report, he specialized in robbing Payless shoe stores: "After visiting the shoe stores and making himself known to the clerks, he would return at closing time, rob the clerks at gunpoint, and on some occasions rape a female clerk."

The phrasing of "and on some occasions" in relation to rape has stuck with me for its relaxed, minimizing candor.

My father went to the arraignment. He thought this was a type of revenge—something to bring him peace. I had no such illusion. I stayed home and watched the Olympics.

On August 1, Gail Devers took her place in lane 2 at the women's one-hundred-meter dash. Her medical history had made her one of the big Olympics stories leading up to this first race. Just a year before, side effects of treatment for Graves' disease—an autoimmune disorder of the thyroid—had made her feet so swollen that her doctor told her that if she had walked on them for even two more days, she would have had to have them amputated.

"And here she is," an announcer said. *There she is,* I thought. Her braids were in a ponytail, her brown skin beautiful in the light. I'd already been struck by the women on the USA track and field team, none of them shape-shifting into the smallness of Black American humility. They all had braids, long nails with vibrant colors, outfits cut to win . . . and they were loved.

The eight women took off, racing to a photo finish in the time it took me to take a breath. The winner was Gail Devers, the woman who once could barely walk. Watching her victory lap, I felt that pull again on my heart.

"A lot of times in athletics and in life you feel walls closing in and you can't get out," she said at the press conference afterward. "Use me as an example. If you believe in yourself, if you have faith in yourself, you can do anything."

The walls had not just closed in on me—the very foundation I'd built my life upon had crumbled beneath my feet. Gail Devers extended her hand, invited me to walk on the uncommon ground of excellence. Not just taking steps we thought we never would again, but running. Competing to be great.

That night my mother sat on the edge of the couch and gingerly brought up the family reunion. On her side, we are part of the Bryant-Fisher lineage, the largest Black extended family in Nebraska. We set down roots in the state in 1902, when Emma Early Bryant-Fisher moved to Omaha as a single mother twice widowed. The second Sunday of every August, all the branches of the family—the "Dozens of Cousins"—gathered in Omaha for what we called a picnic, but it's a festival. She wanted to go with my older sister, Kelly. She didn't pressure me to go, but there was an unspoken invitation for me to come along.

I nodded. I couldn't possibly think that far ahead.

Five days after she won the gold medal, I watched Gail Devers start in the hundred-meter hurdles. *Here we go,* I thought. I was with her in the lead. Then, on the tenth and final hurdle, she fell, dragging her foot. She somersaulted into the finish line, coming in fifth. They showed the footage over and over again, reveling in the failure of it all until the shock of the fall was gone. But I only saw the last frame of the slo-mo: when she got up on the two feet she'd almost lost.

———

The Dream Team played their last game the day before the closing ceremonies. The actual game, a rematch with Croatia and Kukoč, was a formality. A setup, really, for the medal ceremony. "I am here and I am dominating," each man said to me as they played, so skilled they basically took turns at the basket so each could score in a gold medal game. "You are going to see me be great." They didn't make that greatness easier to swallow to represent their country. Each would be his full self. Maybe *I* could be my full self, too. That's the message that was building in my head.

During the medal ceremony, these men showed such camaraderie when so much of the world, and certainly the United States, was so frayed, openly rejecting people with HIV and discounting the value of the lives of Black Americans. And here were these Black men embracing *each other*. The idea came to me, small at first, that we can't save each other, but perhaps together we share the keys to our own salvation. When we see each other, embrace each other's greatness, that is freedom, the freedom to be.

It was a small idea, but it had room to grow without that heavy cloak of respectability constricting me. I wanted to be part of something like that. I wanted to be with family.

"I'll go with you," I told my mother. "To Omaha."

She nodded. "Okay."

The Dream Team, Gail Devers, all these Black Olympians, they were the ones who modeled what it could be like for me to take those first wobbly steps out of the house.

The trip remains hazy to me. When we got to Omaha, it was the first time that I was able to connect with my aunts, my dad's sisters. The first time I wasn't just a kid dragged along looking at people as if they only existed in those moments, the way a kid sees a teacher or a doctor. They were not supporting players, but the leads in their stories.

Our second day there, one of my aunts made a joke, I don't remember what, but it must have been a dirty one because before I knew it I was laughing. And the surprise was so great, I laughed again.

Originally, I wanted to end this story in Omaha, in the hope that I could move this ghost of involuntary memory to some place safer. Let her go from my parents' living room and leave her to sit in the August sun with her people.

It would be an apology of sorts. I felt bad that I had walked in on her when she was so vulnerable. She'd been there alone for nearly thirty years, and it felt awkward to intrude on her space, even though she was me. I've grown accustomed only to the two mes. The one before the rape and the one I had to create to survive. But I forgot this third girl, the one in between. The one who existed solely to get me from one life to another.

All she had was what the Olympics gave her, and I know now the message she took in and handed to me as a guide wasn't quite right. I could be Black and excellent—yes. But I also thought that if I was just great enough, everyone would love me and root for me. What I didn't learn until later was that I am free and deserving simply because *I exist*. I don't have to do all these other things to be worthy of respect and safety. Greatness is not required. It took a long time to undo that belief, but I understand she needed any lifeline she could grasp to get off that couch.

It's been almost three decades since I limped away from that living room, but that nineteen-year-old remained there with her story untold. I can't close the door on her again, and go on about my life. The right thing to do is, as usual, the hard thing to do. I was foolish to think I could leave her sealed off to haunt my parents' house in Pleasanton, or even to tidily move her to Omaha for safekeeping.

Finally, I have to accept that her ghost is here with me, and always will be. She is me.

3

EMBRACE YOUR KRYPTONITE

He sat across from me, regarding me for a long time. "You know . . ." he started.

Let's get this out of the way: a couple of years ago I was in a consult with a shaman. Yelp actually has a list of the "10 Best Shamans in Hollywood," but that is not how I found him. Laugh, but I got results. Like what he was about to tell me he could see in my aura.

"You look at vulnerability as your Kryptonite," he said.

Correct, I thought, and nodded.

"And you need to think of it as your superpower," he continued. "Vulnerability will unlock everything that has been denied you. If you can be emotionally open and transparent—with yourself and others—you will have everything you have ever dreamed of."

Shoot, I thought. There went everything I ever dreamed of. But I nodded again like I believed every word.

He knew I was lying. Can't shit a shaman. "No," he said. "These qualities don't make you weak. They make you strong."

I bluffed, talking about it clinically, like I was someone else assessing my criminal profile in a thriller. "The subject has an intense fear of public humiliation and views any displays of vulnerability as an invitation to harm her. Look here, you can see where she cauterized the wounds herself. Subject is also aggressively allergic to needy people. It's quite a miracle she can feel anything, really."

The shaman was the first person to explain to me that to be vulnerable doesn't mean you're weak. And if you've let people into your life who have attacked your vulnerability, it's not because you exposed some Achilles' heel, it is absolutely a deficit in them. When you acknowledge that your vulnerability does not absolve anyone of personal accountability, you will heal from those traumas faster and more fully.

As I opened myself up, a shift naturally happened—one I had never anticipated. I gradually became more nurturing, drawing on a feminine energy I had always discounted. To me, womanliness meant giving without an expectation of reciprocity, just the hope of gratitude. I thought it was asking to be dominated or made a fool of. My mother has a nurturing nature, and my father cheated on her for years. I wouldn't allow that weakness in my own marriage. In the past, when I impulsively showed some softer, maternal side to Dwyane, he would immediately respond with love. But I would quickly check myself and bat it away. Dismiss it with a joke before anyone, even my husband, thought I was going soft. Gradually, I stopped myself from resisting this nurturing side of myself. Dwyane and I formed a deeper connection, and there was a shift in the energy of how I moved in the world. Everyone noticed, from friends and coworkers to the kids.

Especially the kids. I always get a lot of credit for being a stepmother, right? It's part of our Hollywood story: D got full custody of Zaire and Zaya, and then his nephew Dada, shortly after we started dating. The weekend dad became a full-time dad, and I made a commitment to be a present, consistent *adult,* never a mother figure. The real moms were in Chicago. I was careful in interviews to always refer to "the kids," never, ever "my kids," and when reporters would press me with "What do they call you?" I was ready with a pat, "Nickie. It's what my family calls me. From my middle name, Monique."

That's really why I get a lot of said credit. I was very vocal and public about knowing "my place." And I defined that "place" by what I was most certainly not: their mother.

But what was that place, really? When I was around, I didn't know what my job at home entailed. Though each child is different, each needed some form of mothering. Not someone to replace their mothers, but nurturing energy in the home. I never knew how to maneuver that. If I stepped in, I worried I could be seen as a presence for their mothers to have to fear. This created an emotional barrier between me and the kids. Not quite a wall, but a fence. They knew I was close enough that I was not gonna let them hurt themselves doing something crazy. I would support their extracurriculars, be the one to go to speak to school administrators when I had to remind them about implicit bias and treating these Black children fairly and with respect. Yes, I would be there to help as I was called upon, but always stay far enough away that no one who's peeking could ever accuse me of stepping over some invisible—and kind of impossible—boundary. "See this fence?" I could say, my hands where they could see them. "Nickie. Not the mom. I know my spot."

When we all moved to California in the fall of 2019, that distance began to trouble me. With Dwyane retired, and me not traveling as much for work after Kaavia James's birth, this was the first time we really lived together as a family unit. Issues are harder to ignore, and Zaya had something come up. We were in the living room, and I knew she had been hurting about something for days. I remembered being thirteen and keeping things to myself. Usually, I could flag something to Dwyane and dispatch him to look into it. But he was away on business.

For days, I found reasons just to be around, hoping Zaya would say something. I told myself that she knew I was there, and she could come to me if she had to. But why should she have to wait until "she had to"? Not in the sense of me being a last resort, but why should she have to find the ability to verbalize that she was vulnerable and in need of help when I was only just learning how to do that myself? Instead, I could just offer that help freely.

I took a breath, and blurted it out before fear stopped me. "My desire, my inclination," I said softly, "is to run in. Hold you and hug you and let you know that it's going to be okay."

Zaya gave me a receptive look. I admitted to her that I had always put up a fence between us. That I had cared so much about the risk of some imagined stranger snapping that I was overstepping a boundary. Of course, Zaya knew the difference between me and her mother. I was giving away all my power to some unseen watcher in the woods.

She shook her head, and looked away. "I feel like I've had three childhoods," she said. She explained that there was the one when she was mostly with her mom until she was three years old. Then the one with her nanny while her dad played in the NBA. "And then the one with you and Dad. Watching you guys with Kaav, I'm seeing what a childhood could have looked like."

Those words broke my heart, and I let it break. I let myself acknowledge her pain, and feel my own in return.

"I'm not gonna wait any longer," I said. "With your permission, I'm gonna storm through the fence. I'm gonna be the Nickie that you need. And while I'm not your mother, I can mother you well."

This felt dangerous, and it felt necessary. We hugged the kind of soul hug I would have resisted before I started this vulnerability work on myself. And the work continues. Vulnerability is not only a journey, it's the opposite of perfection. I still catch myself and sometimes hear the echoes of what my parents taught me as we are raising Kaavia James.

Like all good parents, I would like to avoid messing up my kid, so they don't have to unlearn habits later. But they start so early, like sponges soaking up all the details. Right now, at a year and a half, Kaav is in a stage where she doesn't want to wear pants. Fine, it's summer and it's not a battle I'm fighting at home. So, her legs are forever bare. She is also a runner, and the more a kid races around, the more they are likely to fall. The outside of our house has a concrete area, and you'd think that maybe when she is running top speed she would say to herself, in a thoughtful baby voice, "Oh, I was running really fast in this spot last time and I fell, so maybe I should . . ." Nope, full speed ahead.

Yesterday we were all outside by the pool, watching her run around with her little romper on. She was running with her back to us when she fell forward to the ground. Everyone froze. Parents will tell you, "When kids fall, don't react. Because however you react to them falling is really them reacting to you." I bought into that, lock, stock, and barrel.

"Get up," I said. "You're okay." She did get up, and did not cry. But when she turned, we saw she had completely skinned her knees.

"Oh, God," I said. We scooped her up to bandage her, but I thought about the more lasting damage. I had just told her what her feelings were. Even when she was legitimately harmed and had to have felt real pain, I negated her feelings. She told herself she was fine even though she was bleeding. Otherwise, somebody might think she was soft. I ignored her vulnerability.

Is this how it started with me? My father's definition of endurance, which he drilled into me, was not acknowledging real pain. Tears were weakness, and nobody wanted to see that. "Toughen up. Toughen up." That was how you were supposed to raise kids so they'd be equipped to handle every adversity life could throw at them. What kind of message was my one-and-a-half-year-old processing? "I know I'm bleeding, but they're totally silent. And my mom told me to get up and nothing's wrong. And if someone you love tells you how you feel, you should take their word for it."

A tricky part of parenting is finding that balance between being a hoverer and being dismissive of real pain. At a certain point we all know our kids and know when they are reacting to our reactions and when they are in real pain. We should be reminding ourselves that expressing hurt or articulating whatever pain they may be feeling—emotional, spiritual, sexual—is not only okay but encouraged. You can teach resilience without "toughen up, kid." That proverbial stiff upper lip can actually be nurtured through encouraging people to communicate, rather than instilling a fear of emotional connection and vulnerability. Articulating your feelings, whether they be about pain or joy. Clearly, the goal should be effective communication, not the shutdown of feelings.

"You're fine" is a pretty short con. It will only last a few years, because if you tell a smart kid they're fine and they know better, they won't communicate their fears and hurts to you later, when it's not about skinned knees. Because by then they will see through you saying, "You're fine." They will say, "You cannot be trusted." Those teens then become grown-ups, who will then internalize the external—people's reactions, behavior, decisions—and prioritize them. Those teens become me, sitting across from a shaman, if they're lucky, learning something they should have been taught when they were Kaav's age.

Once she was bandaged, Kaav got right back out there. No lesson learned, at least about running. I thought it was a pretty good sign that I wasn't beating myself up about what I'd said to her. How wrong I'd gotten it. *Let's see if we can do better next time,* I thought.

See? Growth.

4

ON THE COMPASSION
OF STRIPPERS

It was 3 A.M. in Atlanta, so of course I was taking people to Magic City. When I was in town working, it was the place to go if you wanted to keep the party going after leaving the club. Strip clubs are always there for you in times of such need. In Miami, you had choices: Rollexx, King of Diamonds, Tootsie's, or Pink Pussycat. But in Atlanta, it was always Magic City.

I might have been showing off that night. I was with Chaka Zulu, a successful music exec, and Hype Williams, the iconic video director. We'd just left Compound, and I knew Magic City would greet me with an "Our girl Gab is back!" on the mic.

Ah, but you see, that night I was also constipated. And had been for as long as I'd been in town shooting *Daddy's Little Girls*. It is hard to feel like a bad bitch when you're so backed up you feel nauseous.

On the way to Magic City with the windows down and the music up, we stopped at a gas station. I saw they had a convenience store, and had a eureka moment fired by drunk logic from brown liquor.

"Yo, I gotta go in and grab something," I said. *If I take it now*, I thought, *I should be good to go in the morning*.

Yes, Ex-Lax. When I found the chewable chocolate kind right away under the too-bright fluorescent lights, it seemed the universe was giving my plan a thumbs-up. Just as I brought it to the register, Hype walked in behind me to get a water. I quick-grabbed a magazine to buy and throw over the little blue-and-white box of deliverance. Just some light reading material for the strip club, nothing to see here. The man who'd revolutionized music videos with Michael and Janet's "Scream" and Missy's "The Rain (Supa Dupa Fly)" was not going to catch me buying laxatives at a gas station. With yet another remarkable sleight of hand, I sneak-gobbled up a couple chocolate pieces on the way to the car. I prided myself on my forethought as we took off for Magic City downtown. My morning self would be so pleased with my nighttime brilliance.

In the study of film, Hitchcock's "bomb under the table" theory of suspense boils down to the audience knowing that in fifteen minutes a bomb will explode beneath the characters. They then go on about their business, talking about trivial shit while the audience watching becomes increasingly frantic, on the edge of their seats, desperate to warn them.

Well, I was sitting on a time bomb, and I wish you'd been there to warn me.

But for the moment, I just wanted to continue the party. I knew Magic City would deliver a good time. It was one of my favorite strip clubs, and I had become something of an expert in the genre. They'd been there for me in good times and bad. A few years before, I was miserable in Montreal filming *Abandon,* a movie so bad I just now had to Google myself with "Katie Holmes" to remember the title. I was stuck there for three and a half months of shooting, and my part was so small that if you shot all my scenes in a row the time would have amounted to six days. I felt the producer, Lynda Obst, was mad at me for not moving the date of my wedding after they changed their shooting schedule. It appeared she didn't understand why I couldn't reschedule a destination wedding for 350 people. This was my first wedding, one I didn't really want to have, but, still . . . The irony is I'd actually taken the job to cover the costs of the wedding that I had to pay for completely on my own. As a concession, I gave her the time I had allotted for my honeymoon. But that was not enough of a sacrifice. I was kept there in Montreal on call to work at any moment, though I wouldn't be needed for weeks at a time.

I spent days on end in my hotel across from McGill University, where most of the film was shot. Newly married and separated from everyone in my L.A. life, I fell into a depression. I disappear when I'm depressed, playing a sort of emotional hide-and-seek where I'm never found. But I'd impulsively answered the phone once, probably thinking it was room service, and my girlfriend Essence Atkins heard it in my voice. I think she called me at eight in the morning and was at my hotel by eight that night.

"You have to get out of this room," she said, throwing open the curtains I'd kept closed tight for weeks. "Let's go walk around. I know what'll cheer you up."

She took me to a male strip club. Back home in California, we had a group of girlfriends who were fans of the Right Track, an all-

Black-and-brown strip club in South Central Los Angeles. We went so often, we got tired of schlepping down there, so we started hosting parties at our homes. We'd invite our favorite stripper, Quiet Storm, who was so sweet and never pervy. He'd always start with Aretha Franklin's "Dr. Feelgood," coming out in scrubs and a stethoscope to diagnose the problem. He made tons of money from us because whenever a girlfriend in our group was down, Quiet Storm was the medicine.

There was no Quiet Storm to be found at the club in Montreal, but we made do. In Canada they don't use bills for dollars, they have coins. There was a little something lost in the translation of currencies as I sat there with my stack of coins like Scrooge McDuck. Also, the guys walked around with these step stools, which they stood on to give lap dances directly in front of you. Then some other woman would hold a coin in the air and they'd mosey on over to that person with their step stool. One guy put the coin in the top cleft of his butt cheeks and dropped it out. He was so earnestly sexy about it, but we had to hold in our laughter.

Essence was right—a strip club will cheer me up every time. First of all, at Black strip clubs there's some bomb-ass food. That's always important. At the male strip clubs, the clientele tends to be more of the bachelorette type, even when there's no bride. It's women letting loose, getting to look at fine-ass dudes who have rhythm and amazing bodies. They feel, for some bit of time, that they are the only women in the world. The clientele at those places is mainly women, but at the strip clubs that have women dancers you can have a more mixed clientele—male and female, gay and straight—because it's basically an after-hours club. While the bachelorette girls are having the main event of their night out at the male strip club, here, this is just part of the night. Or morning.

But oh, I hear you, the minutes are ticking by, aren't they? That bomb is going to go off any minute.

When Hype, Chaka, and I got to Magic City, I was again shocked by how small it was. It's a tiny place with no windows, painted white to catch the neon lights shining on it. I was greeted with open arms, Norm at her Cheers, and we were led to my usual spot in the way back, a slightly elevated area catty-corner to the entrance, across from the square ring of the stage. The darkest part of the club, it's where the celebrities sit, except for the ones who want to be seen. We got our stack of money to tip the dancers, dollars shrink-wrapped by the hundreds. At Magic City, the dancers were stars and kingmakers, all Black and of every body type. If they liked a new song you knew it was going to be a hit. Artists came to test out music, even songs in progress, just to see how the women reacted.

Adult dancers have always been kind to me, and it's mutual. I show all love and respect and praise, and it's returned. I always had conversations with the women who danced at Magic City. I wouldn't say I made friendships, but we made connections. There was some-thing about each one of them to compliment, even their hustle. I've heard people say demeaning things like, "You're too good for this," or, "What do you really want to be doing instead of this?" Show me jobs where you can make ten thousand dollars a night. I never asked questions like that.

We settled in, bottles everywhere, the money on the floor like carpet. After a while, a pretty young woman about my age started dancing on me, giving me a lap dance to the Ying Yang Twins' "Salt Shaker." We weren't doing this for the enjoyment of the men around us. This was the give and take of two powerful women. I was moving to the beat with her . . . feeling that groove.

. . . and it hit. The first symptom was a complete flop sweat, like a sudden fever. *Oh no*, I thought. I was, like, crowning. I needed a bathroom or instant death from humiliation. But . . . I have always had a thing about shitting in public restrooms. And I had an idea of how the women's room would be at Magic City—packed to the gills. I was not close enough to my hotel to get back in time.

When she turned to face me, I met her eye and lifted my chin to be closer to her ear. "Um, I'm sorry," I said. "I really, really need a bathroom. Can I . . . can I use yours?"

There was a moment, maybe a half second of stillness in her gaze, even as her hips continued to move. She understood the severity of the moment, and nodded like we'd worked out a plan. She asked another dancer, probably someone junior to her, to collect the money I'd already thrown.

"C'mon," she said, taking my hand to lead me through the club to the stairwell and down to the dancers' locker room. As we descended, the noise of the club dissipated until it was mostly the bass.

"I am so sorry," I said. "I think I did a colon speedball. Jesus."

She turned to laugh, but not in judgment. She opened the door to the locker room, and it felt like I was sneaking into someplace . . . sacred isn't the word, but private. I have been in strip clubs all over the world, and I never once had seen the dancers' personal space.

"Hey, ladies," I said, managing to temporarily still be me even as I sweated and clenched every part of my being. There were about a dozen girls in there, mostly nude, sorting bags of money or getting ready to go back upstairs. G-strings hung on hooks on the wall. They were all excited to see Gabrielle Union popping in to say hi. Some started to come over to hug me, when a woman came out of the tiny bathroom behind me. "I'm just gonna . . ." I started to say, trying to sound casual as I raced in. "I'll be right back."

Oh, God. Once I was safely there, I made sounds like explosions.

There's no getting around it. It was an endless barrage of my body releasing a cauldron of demons. Constant flushing in the hopes of signaling an end. How long was it? Fifteen minutes? Thirty? What day was it now?

Finally, I felt a calm, a tentative easing of relations between my bowels and my soul. I knew I was tying up the one bathroom in their small private space. I had to give these women a chance to pee.

I came out of the bathroom, dreading their faces. Maybe they had fled. But no, there they were. These naked women of every body type. Students, professionals, mothers, and hustlers, young and older. Every kind of woman, staring at this actress, who had a self-induced problem and needed help at that moment in time.

I told them about taking the Ex-Lax, and how it kicked in sooner than I anticipated. I apologized profusely for taking over their lone bathroom. "I know this is your space," I said.

They rallied in sympathy around me, with smiles and head shakes. I sat down, and one woman rinsed a rag in cold water and went to put it on my brow.

"You don't have to—" I said.

"I want to," she said, pressing the rag to my head. I relaxed. Had the roles been reversed, I would have judged someone who came in and took over the limited private space I was allowed at work. But not them. I started cracking jokes, and we shared stories, so many starting with "One time . . ." Because this would someday be a "one time" for me to share.

These women were completely naked and I was at my most vulnerable, living a nightmare of humiliation. You would think we could not be more open with each other than that, and yet they let me in even closer, to the intimacy of compassion.

When I hear people talk shit about strippers, I go back in my mind to the locker room at Magic City. A cold rag on my forehead, telling jokes, and sharing the mercy of true sisterhood. The demeaning myth is that these women must have had something go wrong in their life to be there with me in that moment. An abusive dad, a nasty ex—pick your cliché. But we were all women who made choices, none of us better than the next. I wish I didn't have to emphasize that you can be a "good" woman and do this work. You can be a good mother, a good wife, and work as a stripper.

In that moment, I needed them to be human and to have compassion for me. And they had it in spades. We know that doesn't always happen outside Magic City. People can judge them for what they think strippers are or aren't, but I ask those people: If the time bomb goes off and a person's ass explodes, what kind of woman are you? Will you be there for her? Wouldn't you want someone to be there for you?

5

GOOD SOLDIERS

I dialed my dad's number, realizing I hadn't done so for a while. It was the summer of 2013 and I had been invited to D.C. to stand with Congressman John Lewis as the U.S. Postal Service introduced a stamp commemorating the fiftieth anniversary of the 1963 March on Washington. Congressman Lewis was one of the original Freedom Riders and at just twenty-three he helped organize the march—the start of a life of service. When they asked me to appear alongside him, my immediate answer was, "What? Me?"

Maybe when I called my dad I wanted to brag, but I also realized I didn't know where our family fit in that moment in '63. I am a compulsive planner, and I wanted something to talk to the congressman about, some connection. Two hundred fifty thousand people filled the National Mall to bear witness to what Dr. Martin Luther King Jr. called the greatest demonstration for freedom in the history of the United States. So, where were the Unions in all this? Probably in Omaha, but surely they were on the front lines of change in some capacity. I pictured them sitting in at lunch counters, sprayed by hoses. They raised me to do the right thing, so where were they when it counted?

"Well, uh, I was in the military," my dad said. "We were overseas."

"Hunh," I said. That was right, he would have been nineteen. I had a vague notion that my dad would have been stationed in Europe at the time. "Did they pipe in the speeches?"

"What?"

"Did they have it playing for people to hear?"

He chuckled, and I realized the absurdity of my question. "*They* weren't really wanting us to be involved with that," he said. "The more into civil rights you were, the more they thought you might be radicalized. We might realize, 'Hey, we're here fighting for freedoms that we don't actually have in the United States.'"

I know a lot of us imagine our parents not just on the right side of history, but making it. I didn't do a good job of hiding my disappointment. "Oh, so, did you at least hear it?"

"Oh, sure," he said. "Mainly the Black guys crowded around to listen to it. But you couldn't have a reaction. Couldn't even nod. Otherwise they might think you were a troublemaker."

I pictured telling John Lewis, then the last surviving speaker at the freedom march and the man who popularized the phrase "Good trouble," that my father was not a troublemaker. I don't know what I expected, but definitely not my dad as an impassive statue.

"Okay, cool, cool," I said, hurrying off the phone for my next call. Now, my mom, she *had* to have a story. She was still doing good works in Omaha, full of stories about how she and her friend Father Ken went around ministering to the real-life needs of homeless people and sex workers. Father Ken was considered a rabble-rouser by Catholic Church standards, but they wanted to reach people they thought needed nonjudgmental fellowship. *Surely*, I thought in my loftiest internal voice, *she was up to stuff in 1963*.

"I was in high school," she said.

"Yeah, but things were happening around you, right? You were aware."

"I was aware, of course," she said. "But I was in school."

Sacred Heart Catholic High School was about creating reasonably intelligent ladies who followed doctrine, not change agents. "But still," I said, "what was happening in Omaha at the time?"

"Well, you know, there were sit-ins at the lunch counters and I really wanted to do them," she said. These were acts of passive resistance to protest the criminalization of Blacks utilizing public spaces. "My friend Janet went and she did the sit-in at the Woolworth's downtown."

Janet was one of my mom's best friends. They did everything together. There was no way Janet went somewhere without taking my mom.

"So, where were you?"

"Well, like I said, I *wanted to,* but . . . Grandma said no."

"Grandma said no," I said, deflated.

"Yeah, Grandma said no," she said. "They were televising these things and publicizing the names of people who took part. These were young people, but their parents and family members could lose their jobs. Grandma was like, 'I've got seven kids. I can't afford to lose my job because *you* wanna go sit in somewhere.'"

I had pictured my mother as a Freedom Rider, the one organizing the sit-ins. The cool girl looking back in a black-and-white photo. Maybe not named in a history book, but on a page somewhere.

"So, Grandma said no and that was that," I said.

"Yeah," she said, quick as a breath with no regret. "It's how it was."

"Well, this story sucks," I said, laughing.

"Well, I'm sorry, but it's a true story," she said, meeting my laughter with her own. "We all understood that there was a lot more at stake for the future, but that day my siblings and I needed to eat. We needed to have a home and we needed to have clothes, and we couldn't live without one of our parents having employment. It just wasn't on the table for us."

"I asked Dad and he didn't have anything good, either . . ."

"Did he mention what happened to him in the riots?"

"In Omaha?"

"It's his story," she said, with the voice of someone who'd been divorced nearly two decades. "See if he'll tell you."

I hit my dad's number again and didn't waste time. "So, tell me about your experience with the Omaha riots," I said as a greeting.

He coughed, a little surprised. "Wow, I haven't thought about that for a long time."

I shifted in my seat, ready for a story about my dad leading some brave charge.

"I'd just got out of the military," he said. "Just gotten home. And I was running to the store to get something when the riots broke out." I realized he had to have been talking about the Fourth of July weekend uprising of 1966, when a large group of Black teens stayed out late to escape the 103-degree heat wave, hanging out in the parking lot of the Safeway supermarket. I spent summers in Omaha as a teen decades later, so I know the feel of that oppressive heat. How finding community is sometimes the only way to get your mind off it. Cops came, demanding a dispersal. A fight broke out, and more and more cops showed up who escalated the scene with brutality. It sounds so simple—"A fight broke out"—but of course it was the result of *decades* of brutality against Black people, and corrupt, racist housing policies that choked off North Omaha. Redlining made home loans unavailable to Black people, marking their neighborhoods as hazardous and unworthy of investment. In the distance of streets, not miles, there were two Americas. That July night was just an igniting of years of indignities stacked upon each other, an explosion of violence.

"As I was coming home from the store, police rolled up on me and threw me to the ground," he said. "They had guns on me, and I kept saying, 'I just got out of the military. Army. Army.' Basically, 'I fought for my country. I'm one of the good guys.'"

He paused. "In that moment, it didn't matter."

All that mattered was that he was Black. I pictured him on the ground, groceries strewn next to him. Then back to him listening to the March on Washington, trying not to have a reaction so he could be seen as a good soldier. You can do all that to not be considered a problem, but you can never assimilate yourself out of harm's way.

"What happened?" I said.

"They moved on," he said. "I got up. Went home."

"I'm sorry," I said. "I didn't know that story."

"Yeah," he said. Ready to change the subject. I let him.

My father served his country proudly abroad and got back only to be treated like a criminal. His patriotism didn't matter. The only thing that mattered was he was Black at the wrong time. But when has there ever been a good time to be Black in America?

Throughout my life, my parents were always the ones who took people in. We had aunts and uncles, mine and theirs, come and stay with us while they got on their feet. If you were a cousin or a long-time friend, they would literally take in your kids while you got your life together. Loan folks money, get them a job, pay toward some-one's schooling . . . My mother had a long run in telecommunica-tions, but before and after the corporate world she devoted her life to helping people as a social worker. She started first at a nonprofit community action center focusing on impoverished Black people in Omaha, then as a Child Protective Services worker with a drive to keep families, or at least sibling groups, together. The whole point of her fostering and adopting my three siblings as infants when she was past sixty was to keep them together. My parents found ways to be part of the solution without always having to put their heads on the chopping block.

They didn't get a public acknowledgment for what they did, and they didn't give me a good story to impress people in D.C., but what they did, what they endured, was just as important. When I finally did meet Congressman Lewis, I realized that he probably wasn't interested in talking about what my parents did in some black-and-white montage of memory. His directive, "Get in trouble. Good trouble. Necessary trouble," was, and remains beyond his death in 2020, for the present. What risks am I taking, large or small, with the luxury of privilege that I have?

That's what I think about when I give talks, and inevitably there is someone who raises their hand and meekly asks, "How can I be a better ally even though sometimes I don't feel strong enough to speak out?" I can't snap my fingers and say, "Do it anyway." Espe-cially these days, when so many people's jobs are at risk and they are a hot second from the unemployment line. Not many people feel that luxury of speaking up when they're living paycheck to pay-check, just grateful to have any kind of employment.

Sometimes you see problematic behavior and if you're not comfortable calling it out and being at the forefront, there are other ways to help. When somebody else is brave, back them up. Don't negate their experience or find some means of explanation. Just say the simple phrase, "Yeah, that happened."

It's even better to build up your integrity beforehand. Let people know you are not the one to come to with racist, homophobic, transphobic, Islamophobic "jokes." Don't do the polite chuckle or the quiet "sheesh, that's bad." Be clear that you're not a safe space for oppression. They're trying to give you a secret handshake, hoping for strength in numbers to shore up problematic power. Don't take the handshake.

You can make a difference, and make peace with the fact that not everyone is going to be on the front line. Not everyone is going to get that major, easily identifiable footnote in history.

But we can all do something.

Speaking of footnotes, I have one to share, though again, you won't find it in history books. Last Christmas we went all out on a family photo shoot. Dwyane's mom flew in, and my mom came in, plus my dad and his second wife, my stepmother. We did the shoot in Miami, and in classic Union-Wade tradition, afterward we sat by the water with margaritas and sangria.

When my mom and my stepmom are in the same place, it's always a little odd and tricky for me to have both Mrs. Unions there. We were a couple of drinks in, so past recriminations came up, fortunately not about each other, but about times we had to let someone know we were not with the fuckshit.

My mom leaned back. "You know, I remember when I got this

call that my husband whipped some white man's ass for calling him a nigger."

Dad started cracking up, but the rest of us froze, mainly because my mom said "my husband" which made us all go, "Oop." That was a little too present tense for this crowd. But then I sat up. "Wait, wait. How is it that I am this old in the year of our Lord and I never heard about my dad whoopin' somebody's ass? And, excuse me, I just want to clarify that you said a *white* man's ass?"

Yes, indeed, she did. My dad was working on the line at Western Electric in Omaha in the early 1970s. A fellow employee called him a nigger and that was it, my dad snapped and punched him in the face. The guy reported him to their supervisor, not mentioning the whole racism part, which my father hadn't forgotten.

"Did you call him . . . that?" the supervisor asked the white man, when he learned the full story. When the man nodded and shrugged, trying to proffer that secret handshake, the supervisor didn't take it.

"Well, that's what you get," he said.

My dad called my mother to tell her there might be trouble. I can imagine the pride and fear mixed in the call, back and forth on both ends. He was a worker, not in management yet, but he was going to night school. Still, it was a good job. What would the consequence be for standing up?

We were quiet, the word nigger echoing down decades later. Back then, it was a victory that the man who called him a nigger didn't get him fired or arrested. But that word holds a promise of harm, you just don't know what form it will take—violence, oppression, rage, murder, fear? It's a consuming vortex that can suck the safety from a peaceful night years after it is hurled.

I was struck by my dad's progression then in a, what, eight-year span? From having to be a statue, to being thrown to the ground because your skin was enough evidence of guilt, to whoopin' some-one's ass because that was the last time someone was going to call you nigger.

Maybe I do come from civil rights icons, I thought. *They just do it in their own way.*

6

ZAYA

"I need a picture of just me," Zaya said.

She was in the third grade and we were living in Chicago, where D was playing with the Bulls. I was finishing up my first book and briefly living with the deadly cold of that city before I left town for work again. A real winter was still a novelty for the kids; Zaire and Dahveon were both fourteen, and at nine years old, Zaya had recently made her first ever snowball after living in Miami for years. (A note: At this time, Zaya was ascribed a gender role that was incorrect for her. She accepted he/him pronouns because she did not yet have the voice to request otherwise. When I use her correct pronouns she/her, please know I am not trying to rewrite our shared history, but I do so out of love and respect for her. I will also only use her chosen name here.)

"What do you need a picture for?" I asked.

Zaya already had her smile, an indulgent one that invited everyone else to catch up. In our family of five she was the philosopher with swag.

"For *school*," she said, as if that should be obvious. Her class was set to do an assignment the next day about identity. The kids would place pictures of themselves in the center, then draw spokes coming from the photo with things that people don't know about them.

I got a call from her teacher the next day. On one of the spokes, Zaya had written, "I'm gay."

Again, Zaya lives her life. We catch up. She had not shared this with us directly, but Dwyane and I had started the conversations a few years before. At the age of three, Zaya showed that she and her older brother Zaire did not share the same interests at all. To his credit, Dwyane never pushed a basketball on Zaya once she showed she much preferred gymnastics. Zaya was already so much herself so young that we had prepped for this for years, but still only as a question. Dwyane had asked himself how he would react if his child came home and said she was gay. The test wasn't about Zaya. It was about him as a father. Who was he as a father?

The teacher had called right away because the About Me assignments were made for display at the school's open house. She said she was excited for Zaya, but since this was the first time this news had been articulated, she wanted to be able to respect Zaya's privacy. She said she just didn't know if every parent would be able to appreciate that she deserved privacy. Her teacher added that Zaya said she was going to tell Dwyane and me when she got home from school.

Dwyane was about to leave for practice, and I told him what the teacher had said. He nodded, as he does, taking in the information. It was game time. All the what-ifs were about to be in play. He did what he does when he is focused on what you are saying: he lowers his head slightly, knits his brow, and sets his mouth not to speak until he has considered what you've said. The end result is that he just looks angry.

"I need you to practice your listening face," I said, like a director. "I need open face, eyebrows up, like, 'Oh, this is a pleasant discovery.'"

While D was at practice, I sat on the cream couch in our living room to be there when Zaya's nanny brought her home from school. Zaya took a spot next to me, so small on the huge couch and shaking from nerves. I was nervous, too, trying to make sure my face had the best reaction. These were memories she was going to have forever.

When she told me, I hugged her, and said the words I had prepared. "I'm so happy for you," I said. "Congratulations. This is the best. I'm so happy that you get to live your truth."

Zaya nodded, and I saw a feeling of relief on her face. Not about how I had reacted, but that she had done something she had obviously wanted to do for a while. "So," I said, "are you ready to tell Dad?"

"No," she said, quiet.

I didn't want her to know he knew already. "I think your dad is going to be excited for you," I said.

She said nothing.

When D came home shortly after, Zaya was still next to me on the couch. There is a secret language married people have. *She told me,* my eyes said. *It's on.* D nodded, and took the chair across from the couch.

"So . . ." Zaya said, then fell into me. She tried to find words, starting and stopping until she curled into my body. She couldn't even look at him.

D looked so concerned that I was afraid she would see that "angry" face. I smiled maniacally, trying to imitate a "happy discovery" look for D. *Fix your face.*

He smiled. And finally, she told him.

"I'm gay."

"That's wonderful," Dwyane said. He said her name, and she looked. "I'm so happy for you," he said, looking right at her. "Come give me a hug."

She walked over and fell into Dwyane, and he swooped her into his arms. She had decided in her mind how her dad was going to react and this was the opposite. The fullness of her was held. She cried more, probably a thousand emotions I couldn't begin to guess at happening to her all at once. Her dad was fine. And fine with her being herself.

It was three of us sharing this truth now. "So, who else do you want to know?" I asked.

"Oh, God," she said with a laugh. "Nobody."

"I think people might surprise you," said Dwyane.

"But this is your journey," I said.

I forget whose idea the list was, but I know one of us said, "How about you just give us the names of everyone you *don't* want to know. We'll respect that."

She called it the Never Ever list, naming certain family members who she felt would not respond with immediate acceptance. Zaire and Dada were on the list.

We disagreed with some people on the list, but gave her the agency. "Okay," was all we said.

When the older boys came home and went upstairs, Zaya was on edge, but giddy. She had told someone who works in our home, and she'd gotten such a positive reaction that whatever sad script she had written for this day had been thrown out.

She went upstairs to her room, and came down ten minutes later.

"I told them," she said.

"Who?" said Dwyane.

"Dada and Zaire."

"You *just* put them on the Never Ever list!"

"I know, I know," she said quickly, the star of the show. "I just . . . I just . . . I just told 'em."

"Well, okay," said D, in a protective voice. "How did they react?"

She looked down to get the words exactly right. "Zaire said, 'Oh, okay.' And Dada said, 'Cool.'"

"That was it?" I asked.

"That was it."

"Okay," I said. "Anyone else you want to take off this list? Because people seem to be reacting pretty well." Over the next few days, Zaya told more and more people until eventually there was nobody left on the list. She got, for the most part, reasonable reactions. A few people looked at her age and said, "Maybe you don't want to label yourself too early. You might change your mind."

And things do change as a person accesses more information about themselves and the world around them. Telling someone to be open to change is okay as long as it's not an invitation or demand for silence. Over time, the more we gave Zaya access to her community, the more she realized identity is not about boxes. It's not gay or straight or bisexual. There's a continuum of all sorts of things, where everything that serves you in a healthy way is on the table and nothing is wrong.

In 2017, we celebrated Zaya's tenth birthday in Chicago, and

Dwyane and I each posted photos with her. The world knew Zaya as male. When people detected even the slightest femininity to her carriage, the comments were vicious. It was hurtful that the meanest comments were on Black blogs. They attacked Zaya as a human being, Dwyane as a father, and me as a stepmother. Zaya later told me, "It felt like I was outed, and I was just standing next to my cake."

She was *ten*. It was terrifying, As Black parents, it is almost impossible not to project your fears onto your children. It is sometimes a necessity, having seen the devil up close, and that's the catch-22 of every Black parent: Do you share with your children the reality of the world, or do you allow them to be innocent a little bit longer? And at exactly what point do you strip them of this innocence and reveal the evil and bigotry that exists in the world? How were we supposed to keep Zaya safe, and not rob her of the time to be her most authentic self?

———

It was in the fifth grade, at eleven, that Zaya began voicing her need to wear more feminine clothes. On Target runs, she would pick up pajamas she liked, and began to experiment with makeup the way any young girl would. She identified as gender nonconforming. Because this was a period when we moved a lot for Dwyane's work, at each stop I would visit the school and let them know what was what. We wanted to make sure that the school had an LGBTQ+ community she could be a part of. There needed to be access to mentors and safety.

We were back in Miami in April 2019 when I realized Miami Pride was coming up. I called a place where I had once gone for a drag queen brunch to make an afternoon reservation for the Sunday of Pride.

"This is so crazy," said the manager. "Our float is actually a *Bring It On* float this year. Would you want to come be on our float before the brunch?"

"One, that sounds amazing. I am honored. Two, I just have to check with someone. Lemme call you back."

I hung up and turned to Zaya.

"Would you want to go to Pride and be on this float with me?"

"Oh my God, I've always wanted to go to Pride."

"What? You've always wanted to go to Pride? You've never said anything! I can make any Pride you want happen. Pride is everywhere."

"Oh my God," she said, her hand to her throat, "the *dream*."

I called them right back. "We're in." And we all were. I invited *everyone* in Zaya's support system, and we brought about twenty-plus people to Pride, including her friends, tutors, Zaire, and Kaavia James in her rainbow onesie. Dwyane would have been there, but had to be in Toronto to play the Raptors.

Zaya and I were on the float, and she had her own cheering section forming a circle below us. The whole concept of Pride is the victory of being yourself, because when you are wholly yourself, you win. One of the best moments of my life was on that float, watching Zaya have one of her best moments. I replay it all the time in my mind. Zaya lifts her chin to the air in happiness, safe in the dream she talked about. She is in her community, wrapped in so much love.

We all posted photos on our socials, including Dwyane and Zaire. Dwyane captioned a group photo of the cheering section, "Wish I was there to see you smile, kid." Zaire wrote on a photo of him and Zaya, "Gotcha back, kid." People in the LGBTQ+ community reposted the photos, many saying the images made them cry. This was us being us, just documenting what was already real. It was also an opportunity to say, as a family and a community, "Don't try us. Our belief is stronger than your doubt."

Zaya has called this one of the moments she came out. There was the third grade, then the birthday party in Chicago where strangers pointed and called her gay. And this one, where she came out publicly on her terms. But there would be one more.

———

Just before September 2019, when Zaya was twelve, I was getting ready to go to her new middle school to do my usual "here's the deal." I was on the edge of not being late, but not being early, which I prefer. Dwyane couldn't make it, and I checked in with Zaya right before I left. She was in her room reading.

"Hey, I'm going to go up to the school," I said. "I gotta talk to 'em. How do you want me to identify you?"

"What do you mean?"

"Well," I said, mentioning her old school, "when I met with them, I said you identified as gender nonconforming. A gay boy. Is that still okay with you?"

"Oh, yeah," she said. "I'm not gay. I'm a straight trans girl."

"Okay, great," I said.

Zaya looked back at her book.

As I walked to the front door, I said aloud, "What just happened?" I wasn't shocked, I was just surprised by her nonchalance. I was almost to the car when I ran back inside.

"Okay, um, are you still going by—" I said, using her deadname.

"No, no, no," she said, still so casual. "Um, Zaya."

"Zaya," I said. "Uh, what pronouns?"

Finally, I got her to look up from her book. Her expression said *Really, bitch?* "She and her," she said.

We both started giggling. "Ma'am, *she* and *her*," I said, repeating her. "Well, it's just that there are options. I don't want to assume anything. It could be 'they.'"

She nodded, appreciating my thoroughness. So off I went to the school. Zaya had done a summer program there and had already met so many people using her deadname and he/him pronouns. We had specifically chosen this school in L.A. because we knew other families with gender-nonconforming kids who graduated from there. They had said the community was amazing, but this was our Zaya. It's one thing for people to say "Oh, they're amazing," and it's another thing for people to have to prove it before school has even started. And this was all so new to us, too.

I went in armed and ready with lines I practiced on the way over, but apprehensive. "We need to change all of the paperwork and information to Zaya, which is the name she wants to go by. She is identifying as a straight trans girl. Zaya is her name, and her pronouns are she and her."

"Okay, no problem."

I was ready for a battle.

"No problem." When I tell you I wish this for every parent of an LGBTQ+ child . . . that the person they adore and cherish is not seen as a problem . . . I say this from the deepest part of my soul.

When Zaya started that school, her classmates only knew her as Zaya. From the second she claimed her name and identity out loud, Zaya began to define what femininity meant for her. At twelve, she didn't go for wigs anymore or makeup regularly. She felt she didn't need the cultural trappings of being a girl any longer. She just is.

That realization was profound to me, because I thought back on all that I had been taught at her age about what it meant to be a woman. But much of it amounted to the performance of gender.

My mom showed me how to shave my legs and armpits, and I had wanted to have these bonding stepmother-stepdaughter moments with Zaya. In prioritizing these rites of passage, were we bonding through patriarchy? I felt I would be teaching her what will appear pleasing and thus increase her chances to be chosen by someone else. Not necessarily be *happy* with herself. There's more than one way to be a woman, and I could explain that these were things that a lot of women choose to do, but not all women. "You can be whatever kind of woman you want to be," I told Zaya. "Whoever you are is exactly right, because that's who you are."

I have had to stop myself from rushing in with answers in the form of options. I didn't fully understand the richness of trans identity. That first day coming back from the meeting at school, I assumed that "trans" was about anatomy. I thought I needed to learn about surgery, about hormones. When Dwyane was home, we had a more serious talk with her.

"So, what should we be looking for for you?" Dwyane asked. "Understanding what this means for you."

I said, "Should we be helping you get hormones or—"

"Oh, I'm comfortable where I'm at right now," she said.

"Oh," I said.

"Okay," said Dwyane.

Because, honestly, most of what we knew was from TV and googling. She once asked us, "Uh, you do know there's a difference between gender expression, identity, and sexuality, right?"

We were like, "Yep!" The second she walked away, we were grabbing our phones. "Let's break out the Google," I said. It was hard to shut up and listen. We got her a Black therapist who specializes in LGBTQ+ kids to work out the things she needed to know, but Zaya has always showed us what we didn't know and needed to learn. And she has always led at the pace that is appropriate for her, not us.

At times, we had to catch up. Dwyane and I began discussions that were centered on the ways we and media had decided how trans women needed to move through the world. The impulse was to help her fit in a box. It's so odd to look back on this time, which was not that long ago, and realize how little we were aware that we were foisting our own fears upon her.

We thought we wanted her to be happy. But we wanted her to be chosen. We assumed she had to look a certain way, embrace the typical trappings of femininity, in order to *compete* with other girls. To be deserving of love.

It was an awful, slow realization that made me question my assumptions not just about her but about myself. I realized, finally, having a stepdaughter, why mother-daughter relationships are often so fraught. Zaya is such a reflection of me that I now questioned what I saw in the mirror. What was I giving her to help her grow, and what was I leaving her with to undo?

We have stumbled, but Zaya has not missed a beat. In February 2020, Zaya introduced herself to the world as who she truly is. "Meet Zaya. She's compassionate, loving, whip smart, and we are so proud of her," I wrote in a social media post she approved. "It's ok to listen to, love & respect your children exactly as they are." Dwyane and I said we were leading with love and education, and guaranteed there would be times we took missteps. We wanted to be corrected, strongly and swiftly, when we fucked it up. This was too much truth for some people. There was a large segment of people who always said that I was a real one, a ride-or-die down-ass chick who was deserving of Dwyane's love. And yet our child was not deserving of that same love and acceptance? Instead of compassion and nurturing, our child has experienced trauma, for merely existing, from some of the spaces and people that were supposed to love her the most. Someone, I am not sure why, sent me a story with a headline demeaning Zaya. My mind went to Ntozake Shange's *For Colored Girls Who Have Considered Suicide / When the Rainbow Is Enuf.* What was Zaya supposed to contemplate when the kindness shown her family was snatched quick from her? *For little trans girls,* I thought to myself, *who consider staying in the closet when love and acceptance is too much for some.*

We let Zaya speak for herself when she made her first appearance on the world stage. Dwyane did a golf-cart interview while Zaya was at the wheel, asking her if she had any advice for people who were afraid to be themselves.

"If they're afraid they will be judged, I would say, don't even think about that," she advised. "Just be true to yourself. . . . What's the point of being on this earth if you're gonna try to be someone you're not? It's like you're not even living as yourself, which is the dumbest concept to me. It's just like, Be true, and don't really care what the stereotypical way of being you is."

"Even when people are being mean?" said Dwyane, who I don't think was asking "for a friend" anymore. By then, Zaya had already received so much hate online that it frightened us. "Even when people are getting hurt because they're trying to be themselves?" he continued. "Even through that, you still want people to make sure that they live their truth?"

"Yeah," she said simply. "I think . . . I *know* it can get tough. Definitely. But you push through and you be the best you. . . . It's worth it. I feel it's very worth it. When you reach that point of yourself. You can look at the mirror and say hi to yourself. Nice to meet *you.*"

I often get asked for advice about raising a child in the LGBTQ+ community, and my impulse is to tell them to ask Zaya, since she has taught me so much since that third-grade project. That humility, the sometimes crushing, enforced humility of parenting a new teen-ager, is important. You can tell your child that you don't have the answers, but what you do know for sure is that you love them. Their peace, like Zaya's peace, is not up for negotiation.

And whatever their journey, it will not be taken alone. We're in this together.

7

FRESHMAN ORIENTATION

He has long, pretty eyelashes. I can look at them better because he is starting to fall asleep on the twin bed we are squeezed onto. When you are seventeen, as I am, you see things about people in glimpses until you have the opportunity to really study them. I will forget his name but remember his eyelashes.

We are in his bedroom in his mother's apartment in Newark, California, about a half hour from where I live in Pleasanton. The July sun is starting to rise outside, and I debate whether to wake him so he can drive me home. I will slip in through the unlocked front door and go up to my room with my parents none the wiser. I am wearing one of his old blue Newark Memorial track T-shirts, which someone had done in a book I'd read. Something cute that girls do.

I've put my Umbro shorts back on after a stealth tiptoe to the bathroom, fearful of waking his mother.

The shirt is only "old" because he wore it last year, when he was a senior at Newark Memorial High and I was a junior at Foothill. I know him and his best friend from track meets, and now they both run track for Alabama A&M. They're back home in the Bay Area for summer, and got the coveted jobs parking cars at the Alameda County Fair. Everyone wants the parking jobs because it's all cash. You can park cars illegally, maybe up on the grass, and just pocket the money.

Last night I hung out there with him and his boy at the fair. They are men of the world now after their year in college, full of advice about navigating freshman life and grateful for an audience to their wisdom. College is a year away for me, but I overprepare for everything.

Their advice amounted to this:

"No matter what you do," he told me, "don't fuck anyone in the first semester."

His friend clapped his hands. "For real," he said. "You know . . . the first two months."

My guy nodded. "Get the lay of the land. Otherwise you're gonna get a label. Be tied to somebody or this, that, and the other." He said it again, clapping his hands with each word: "Don't. Fuck. Anybody."

This was not territorial, and I don't care for that to change, even as I am lying in his bed. He is not boyfriend material. But it feels grown-up to be here, wearing his shirt. I realize that this is postcoital bliss, another thing I've picked up from reading.

As I consider how completely unsexy the term "postcoital" is, there is a huge banging sound from the front door. He springs up.

"Oh my God," I say. "It sounds like the police are here."

He is out of bed, grabbing my shirt and stuffing it in my backpack. "They are," he says.

"What?" I say dumbly.

He throws open the screen on the window, and tosses my backpack out. The banging on the front door continues. I stand.

"Run to the Albertson's," he says, scrawling a number on some paper. He tells me to call his friend. "He'll come pick you up."

"What the—"

"*Go,*" he says.

I climb out, lucky that he's on the first floor. My bare feet touch the grass beneath me. "My shoes!" I whisper-yell to him.

My Birkenstocks come flying out the window. I slip them on and begin running to the Albertson's grocery store. His shirt, I decide, is the perfect alibi if I am stopped. "Why am I running?" I say aloud. "I run track. Go Cougars."

The Albertson's supermarket has a Pacific Bell pay phone in its empty parking lot. I find first one dime in a pocket of my backpack, then another. I wake his friend, and then sit on the curb to wait. I am just on the edge of thinking he rolled over and went back to sleep when he drives up. He chuckles when he sees my shirt. He's playing a tape of LL Cool J's *Walking with a Panther,* and I suspect he's cued up "Going Back to Cali" as his song. We head toward Highway 680 to get me home to Pleasanton.

Turns out my guy with the long lashes is a small-time drug dealer. On the half-hour drive, I ask his friend a lot of questions about the business, genuinely curious, but the guy doesn't know much. He steers the conversation back to college, and what I need to know.

"Remember," he says. "Don't fuck anybody."

I am a passenger again one year later, this time in a van my parents have rented for the drive out to Lincoln. It's move-in weekend at the University of Nebraska, a school I have chosen without a campus visit. I have chosen it impulsively, practically out of a hat, to have the decision over with. I give different reasons why, depending on the person.

"I'll be playing soccer there."

"My family actually moved from Nebraska when I was little, so it's home."

"They put me in the international dorm."

I don't yet know that Neihardt Hall is more accurately known as "the nerd dorm." This weekend we are allowed to move our stuff in, but not physically stay in the dorm. So, after moving in, I'll spend the night at my aunt Katie's house in Lincoln, then do orientation Monday.

When I find my room, the door has a sign that my cheery RA made in bubble writing. On it are two names and hometowns: mine and my roommate's, who is not here yet.

"Karen Johnson," I say, as if that will ring a bell. "South Omaha."

"South Omaha," my mother repeats. She has a lightness to her voice, the tentative sound of someone who thinks she might be being recorded. We walk into a small room with two twin beds, two tiny dressers, and two closets.

"Karen Johnson," I say again. My mother nods. Because this name and her hometown both walk that perfect line between whiteness and Blackness. My family is from North Omaha, and we know that while South Omaha has some racists, there are pockets of Blackness. *Karen Johnson*, I think, *could be Black*. And then: *But she could also be white.*

We decorate my side of the room, and when I can't smooth the Bed-in-a-Bag sheets any more to make them look nicer, it's time to go to Aunt Katie's.

"I just wish she could know I'm Black," I say, looking at the bare twin bed next to mine. This feeling or worry has boiled down to the essential matter: It's not whether or not Karen Johnson is white, it's how she will react to having a Black roommate. To sleeping in the same room as me. To sharing a sink with me. Will she object? Will her parents?

It's my mother's idea to leave a picture of myself with a note welcoming Karen to our dorm room. If they are racist, they can see the picture and switch rooms without me having to see them be racist. I can tell myself there was a mix-up. Go on about my life unharmed.

I find a picture of me from a photo album, and place it next to a cheery note. I worry over its placement on the note, angling it just so.

"There," my mother says with a finality, to end this thing we feel we have to do to give someone the opportunity to be quietly racist rather than overtly so. To help them, in some ways, but mostly to spare ourselves the added indignity of having to *witness* that racism.

We leave for Aunt Katie and Uncle John's. She has baked, which she will always be known for. Every year she sends Christmas cookies, and it got to the point that whichever Union was home first would hoard them. She sends us each our own tin now, and promises I will get mine hand-delivered before I go home for Christmas break. "You'll get extra," she says.

Uncle John is a former Nebraska national champion in football, and a real-life action star. He's a black belt in judo who's working his way up the ranks of the SWAT department in Lincoln. He is thrilled I chose Nebraska, and is the one person who doesn't ask me why.

Her kids are around that afternoon. Of all my cousins, we are the most alike in a commitment to sports and academics, but we are not the closest. At the family reunions in Omaha, Aunt Katie's kids hover close by her. Jay, Tanya, Christie, and Taylor are all athletes, but a little too goody-two-shoes for me, even if they are actually good kids. You'll find me and my cousins Kenyatta or Johnny . . . well, you won't find us, because we will be off on some adventure. Tanya and Christie, on the other hand, are not slipping out the window of a drug-dealing hookup.

I spend the afternoon at Aunt Katie's, urging my parents to leave. I blame them for my onset of anxiety, like theirs is contagious. I breathe only in the upper part of my lungs, my chin up like I have to be somewhere. But it's here in Lincoln I have to be. It's only when they are getting in the car that I start bawling. This surprises everyone. I am not that girl. But suddenly I am all elbows and angles in my hugs, pulling on their necks like a child wanting to be lifted up.

When they drive off, I have the feeling I will never see them again. And the question I keep asking myself:

What did I just do?

———

Karen Johnson and her family are moving in when I arrive at the dorm the next day. She is white, and I soon realize she could be the sweetest person ever. She has brown hair and a boyfriend named Dale. Karen's parents act like he is already her husband. We don't have much in common except that she wants to be liked by her college roommate as much as I do.

That first night Karen and I go to a freshman orientation mixer. A mass of eighteen-year-olds trying on new identities to a soundtrack of Color Me Badd and C&C Music Factory. I meet a freshman named William, supercute with dimples and an easy smile. The kind of boy parents like.

"I'm in Neihardt," I tell him, not yet ready to say I live there.

He tells me that he's heard that's the nerd dorm. Toward the end of the night, William invites me to his dorm, which is part of a trio of buildings called Harper-Schramm-Smith. This is where a lot of the athletes live, which at Nebraska means it's where the Black people are. I spend the night with him.

In the morning, I remember the advice of my petty drug-dealer hookup back home: "Don't fuck anybody in the first semester." And here I am on the first day. I've gotten it crackin' and school hasn't even started.

William says, "I'll take you home." When we get downstairs, he leads me not to a car, but to his ten-speed. I stand there for a minute, wondering if I'm supposed to borrow it.

"You can sit on the handlebars," he says.

The ride of shame, I think, but do not say. As he pedals, I sit up there, trying to look cool in day-old clothes. It's like something out of *My Girl,* only Anna Chlumsky's Vada and Macauley Culkin's Thomas J. were eleven. And Anna had her own damn bike.

———

In October, it's William who takes me to my first real college party, a takeoff on the Pajama Jammie Jam in *House Party 2* with Kid 'n Play. Actually, his friend Scott takes us in his black El Camino. There had been a discussion on how to sneak liquor in, so since there is a pajama theme, I use my shower caddy as a giant mixing bowl. We somehow get ahold of Key Lime Mad Dog 20/20 fortified wine and margarita mix, and Karen helps me mix it in our dorm room sink.

When Scott drives up with William to pick me up, they look at me standing there in my pajamas, holding a covered bucket of neon-green alcohol.

"Those are the pajamas?" William says, as Scott laughs. I look down at the pink-and-gray PJ set my mom got me at a department store. The pants balloon out and the loose long-sleeved top is the kind of thing that you wear when it's going to be a bit chilly, but not too.

"What? These are my pajamas."

"Nothing," says William, staring at the floor.

When we get there, I get it. All, I mean *all,* of the women are wearing sexy pajamas, not their actual pajamas. They have the satin and silk jewel tones of TLC's "Red Light Special" while I have the Kmart blue-light special.

"Oh, God," I said. "I'm wearing little-kid pajamas." But my shower caddy makes me popular with the rest of William's teammates. The cool ones are all older, and when you're eighteen, people who are twenty-one or twenty-two look grown. William and I are just playing at being grown-ups.

William seems more childlike to me, and soon after that night, we are at a fast-food place when I offer to get the sodas.

"Get me a stwawbewwy soda," he says.

It's the voice of a three-year-old. Just that word. *Stwawbewwy.*

You can either have a ten-speed bike, or you can pronounce strawberry as "stwawbewwy." But it can't be both. Pick a struggle. And that was the end of William.

A week later I am halfway through an anthro class in a huge lecture hall. Somewhere between analyzing social structures and dynamics, I look over to see a guy checking me out. I look away, then back to find he is still looking. But now he has a sly, wicked, perfect smile. He also has a mustache and a short high-top fade.

When class is over, I move in slow motion to give him time to come over. He does, and he is even cuter up close.

"There you are again," he says, "with the same smile each day."

I give him the look of someone practiced at hearing lines. I am not. I fall for this. There is no hook, no line, no sinker. I basically jump into his fishing boat. He asks if he can know my name, and if he can take me out sometime. Yes, and yes.

Marcus is a sophomore and drives a Renault. He may as well have a French accent because I think that car makes him seem so worldly. I become an ambassador's wife. "Should we take the Renault?" I say about a trip to Amigos, the taco chain.

"Tonight is yours, lady," he says. "Yours and mine."

It is noon. I don't care.

Eventually I will realize that all of his lines were stolen. He was a Magic 8-Ball of Jodeci lyrics, each one he pulled out making just enough sense to be plausible and sexy. This will come to me when a friend plays the *Forever My Lady* album in her car, and for a split second I will think it's so weird that Jodeci copied Marcus. But for now, I think he is a genius of love.

He plays basketball and I go to a preseason game. I am in the stands, thinking about something poetic Marcus had said that day—"Forever my lady, it's like a dream"—when a girl attempts to pass me and does her best to bang into my knees. She comes by again, and this time I see her coming so I exaggerate pulling in my legs. She goes so out of her way to smack my legs that she almost falls on my lap.

"What?" I say.

She scowls at me.

At about 2 A.M. that night the phone in my dorm room rings. I turn on the lamp between my bed and Karen's. "Hello?"

"Meet me at the fountain," a girl's voice hisses. "I'mma whoop your ass."

Now, I had a girl in high school who liked to call and threaten to kill me over a boy. So, I think this might be her.

"Queeshaun? Are you kiddi—"

"*What?* This is Dawn. Oh, shit." She pauses, then hangs up.

I turn to Karen, who looks terrified. "Do you know a Dawn?"

"I don't think so."

"Homicidal Dawn? No?"

"No." She laughs. We turn the light back off, but neither of us can sleep.

"Can I ask you a question?" she says.

"I'm up," I say.

"When we moved in . . . why did you leave a picture on your bed?"

"Oh," I say. "Um, in case you were racist. If you switched rooms, my parents didn't want me to see you be racist."

"Wow," she says.

I don't say anything, and I wonder what she must be thinking. Finally, she says it:

"My parents just thought you were vain."

We roar with laughter.

———

Marcus certainly knows a Dawn, though only in the past tense. They dated through his freshman year, but he insists it was nothing.

It was certainly something to *her*. Through November, she calls me in the middle of the night. Always the same lines, a request to meet me at some university landmark to kick my ass. She could have done a campus tour. She continues to call me even after I have friend-zoned Marcus when his Jodeci plagiarism comes to light and kills the mood.

Karen is good-natured about the after-midnight calls, but she is good-natured about everything. She seems to love it here. And I . . . don't. I love being a Cornhusker, and I love Nebraska, but I am homesick. Not for home, but for experience. All of my friends who stayed in California are having so much fun together. I'm having fun, but not *that* kind of fun.

They send me mix tapes, and I play them alone in my room. I know I am missing out on something. I am all alone, not in a car with them singing to the radio with the windows down after a night at the teen clubs. Back home, I had access to all of the Bay Area and its diversity, which there is a near complete lack of here in Lincoln. I am not imagining this. In a couple of years, the university will begin publishing statistics on undergrad enrollment by race. They will count 373 Black students and 16,122 white students that year. And for the most part, the only Blackness I see here is tied up in being an athlete. I've already dated two of them. In the first semester, no less. There was *one* rule!

Just before I go home for Thanksgiving, the temperature in Lincoln dips to the teens. When I get to California, it's in the sixties and feels like summer. My girlfriends hug me and we have epic nights out. I am in the back of a car that weekend, buzzed. I practically volunteered for the middle seat—the "sitting bitch" spot reserved for newcomers—because I am so happy to be squished between my friends. On the freeway we sing Paula Abdul's "Rush Rush" at the top of our lungs.

When I return to school I work out a plan to leave the University of Nebraska. I will enroll at Cuesta College in San Luis Obispo, California, for the second semester of my freshman year, then transfer into the UC system. Work-study would help me take care of my in-state tuition. It doesn't occur to me until much later that this is one of the first times in my life I've ever wanted to be happy more than I wanted to be right. I decide, if any high school girl ever asks me for advice on freshman year, I will tell her this: "Fuck whoever you want, and follow your joy."

I count the days until winter break. My roommate Karen helps me pack up, and soon my side of our room is completely bare. My cousin Jay comes to drive me to the airport in Omaha and we pack everything in his truck. When I come back to the room for one last goodbye, Karen and I hug. We have done this a dozen times today, but we do it again anyway. We promise to keep in touch, and we do.

"If Dawn calls," I say, "tell her the bitch moved."

"I will," she says.

"Wait. Let me." I dial Dawn's name from the campus directory, and I'm disappointed when she doesn't pick up. When her answering machine begins recording, I start in on a Salt-N-Pepa song that's a perfect goodbye:

"I'll take your man whenever I feel like it," I sing. "This ain't a threat or a bet, it's a damn promise." Before I hang up, I add a final *"Bitch."*

I run out to Jay's truck. Later, Karen will say that I had barely been gone five minutes before Dawn came flying into the dorm. "No one knows who let her in," Karen will tell me. "But she even searched under your bed. 'Where is that bitch? Where is that bitch?' "

Dawn misses her chance, for I am on my way to the airport in Jay's truck. There is a bag at my feet I don't recognize.

"Oh," says Jay, "my mom wanted you to have these."

I reach in and pull out a giant tin of Aunt Katie's cookies. All for me. I open it to take a bite, then another, humming Salt-N-Pepa to myself.

8

THE AUDACITY OF AGING (WITH HOPE)

I'm in love with my husband. I say that not to brag, but to explain why, on an afternoon when we have the house to ourselves, I find myself on the couch with him, laughing at an inside joke we have shared too many times to still be funny. And yet it is. Playing around, I go to straddle him. I'm the whimsical woman in the jeans commercial, the cool girl from Instagram. She's fresh! She's fun!

Krick-crack-ke-crick-crack.

Every bone in my left ankle cracks, not in pain, just in an exhale of effort. Old joints and stiff tendons rubbing against each other to create an unexpected fart of age.

We both freeze in a pose that one second ago appeared playful and now looks like a pharmaceutical ad.

"Damn," Dwyane says quietly, trying to sound deadpan and mournful. "I thought we'd have more time."

This is his recurring joke: the idea that we are outrunning my age, the nine-year gap between us that can feel like the literal time bomb built into our marriage. Sometimes the joke is funny, and sometimes it's fucking not. This day he gets away with it because the moment truly is so absurd. Less so when we are intimate and I catch a full-body cramp. A veteran player like me has gotta keep a banana and some Gatorade handy.

I get why he thinks the joke is funny, because I have always used humor myself to deflect any insecurities about our age difference. If I don't acknowledge it quickly in a public forum, there is a legion of people waiting to beat me to the punch. Check any recent magazine article about "Older Women, Younger Men"—we are usually the stand-by Black celeb couple. They run a Mona Lisa smile photo of me smirking next to Dwyane with a button saying "10 years apart!" For the record, we are technically only ten years apart for two and a half months out of the year, but a decade sounds like a wider chasm than nine years. Especially for an older actress, whose age is measured by the media in dog years.

So, I joke about my back pain during our dual workouts, doing "a bit" where I walk slow and press my palms against my lower back. I always think it hides the fact that I actually *have* to do this, because my back really did start to hurt in my mid-thirties, around the time we started dating. *I must have pulled something*, I thought at thirty-five. The backaches never left, but neither did Dwyane.

At the time, not only did I need to get to know this twenty-six-year-old guy, I was getting to know my body as it began to change, always surprising me with some new development. Early in our relationship, I was at his place, lying with my head across his legs, looking up at him. Millie Jackson was singing on the stereo, then Minnie Riperton's "Lovin' You" came on. It was that early honeymoon period, where you are weighing the pros and cons of forever versus a fun time.

I could get used to this face, I thought, as Minnie did her la-la-la-la-las. Then I saw his gaze move down *my* face to my chin.

"Oh," he said. "You've got a little eyelash . . ."

He went to blow it off my chin, and I felt a light breeze on my face as a quizzical look crossed his.

In that split second, I thought, *That's no eyelash.* This guy was about to huff and puff and he was not gonna move the hair on my chinny-chin-chin.

"Let me get it," he said. In slow motion I saw him reach for my chin. I went to bat him away but he got to the hair before me. He pulled at it, and I felt an unmistakable tug on a firmly established *root.*

"Oh my God," he said in a gasp.

I jumped up and raced to the bathroom as Minnie's soprano whistle echoed through his place. There it was in the mirror, this long hair that I definitely had not seen planting its flag of age on my chin the night before. I opened his medicine cabinet, feverishly searching for a pair of tweezers in a bachelor pad bathroom that basically offered toothpaste and deodorant. "Pesky" did not begin to describe this hair. My eyes welled up in the mirror as I pulled it, suddenly feeling like Cicely Tyson dating Timothée Chalamet. Call me by your name, but loud into my good ear.

What I didn't realize at the time was that this was the start of the hormonal changes that all women face. *Overnight* I could grow a hair damn near an inch out of the middle of my forehead. Or my boob. I became obsessive about gray hairs, staying ever vigilant to dye them. As women, we are trained to see all these little signs of aging come up as a loss, each one a plank disappearing from the rope bridge falling apart behind us. If you dare look back at the young version of you standing back there on the other side—she's the one absently waving, while devouring a Taco Bell Chalupa Supreme after another all-nighter—you risk not being able to do what almost every woman-focused ad and magazine commands you to: outrun age with every bit of energy you can muster.

We are simply not allowed to age in this time of innovation. I saw an article about a new beauty regimen that will literally change the order of your DNA to make you appear more youthful. The writer began the article, "While nothing can be done about *chrono-logical* age . . ." and I laughed. Time is a problem yet to be fixed. The writer cited a new study with promising results for "younger skin," one that had been cited in a science journal called *Aging Cell*. I pictured a call from my publicist. "Guess who wants you for their December cover?! *Aging Cell!*"

You wonder which a scientist would go for, given a choice: Rearranging DNA to help women live longer, or look younger longer? I know which one *I'd* buy stock in, at least. We can try all we want—literally change the genetic codes that make us who we are— but there is a saying in sports that Dwyane repeats: Father Time is undefeated. That Dwyane was a professional athlete actually helped balance the difference in our ages. He'd had a tremendous amount of life experience just having been a teen parent, and was already introspective due to the effects of growing up in extreme poverty with addicts as parents. That work on himself—not to mention worldwide fame and outsized wealth—fast-forwarded his life to a point that made it hard for him to relate to people his age. He gravitated to friendships with older guys . . . and then there was me, Grandma

Moses. The stereotype is that dating a younger man makes a woman feel youthful. No, I felt *matched*. He'd been through so many lives by the time we got together that it felt like he was ready for some stability. And I was in that same place. We could learn from each other, and I held on to hope that someone so young could look at me as someone deserving of love and protection.

But there are moments, right? The foot cracking, the unexpected hair. Or the times I hung out with his younger teammates and realized I was older than their parents. And, of course, the look I read on people's faces when they realize that near-decade difference between me and Dwyane. The glance at him, and then back at my face for lines. There's a taking of accounts before they leave me with the question: "What do you think you deserve for having the audacity to age?"

Because when you go into any relationship, there is an agreement on terms. If someone behaves poorly and the relationship breaks up, there is a general consensus on what the injured party deserves. I'm not talking about money or damages, but compassion. Understanding. However, it seems to be a truth universally acknowledged that when an "older" woman is the injured party, she should have known better. That she signed some sort of waiver entering the relationship dispensing with any right to being blindsided or hurt when it doesn't work out. Not if, but *when*.

It's the "What did you expect?" caveat, which roughly translates to, "Of course you knew, you old bitch, that at some point the gig was gonna be up."

Recently, a friend of mine was legitimately shocked to find out her younger husband was no longer in love with her after years together. They'd had kids together. He swore he was excited to be a young dad, and now he was abruptly bowing out. As she broke the news to our circle, you could hear her tempering her bewilderment and hurt until she just presented a sad resignation. This was just another plank falling away behind her as she aged.

At a catch-up dinner with our group, I could tell she was very aware of the "What did she expect?" talk, even among our circle.

"Yo, I hear you," she said after one too many veiled "Well . . ."'s around the table. "I felt the same way. I asked him repeatedly when we got together, 'Are you sure this is what you want? Because I have already experienced everything that we're about to live together and I don't ever want to feel like I'm robbing you of sharing a first time with someone.'"

She took a sip of wine. "Of course, he was like 'No, no, no . . .'" she said, doing a dead-on impersonation of husbands that only wives can do after waking next to them for years. "Cut to: 'Hey, I don't want to spend my youth just being a dad, watching you be underwhelmed because you've already experienced this shit.'" She paused. "Underwhelmed. I wasn't *underwhelmed*. It was life."

There was a chorus of "that is so awful" at the table, but I knew many of those same people couldn't help but think that she had signed on for this by choosing him. And maybe they thought I had, too. Someone looked at me, but quickly looked away when I turned my face to her.

Our friend collected herself, seeming to remember her lines. "He said he was cool with a woman who was so much older. Raising a family. And at some point . . ." she said, putting her fingers on the stem of the wineglass, to move it just so. She exhaled. "He changed his mind. And that's okay. It sucks, I love him . . . but I get it."

She was so convincing I almost believed her. She was honoring the contract. No matter what cruel fuckery that person got up to, she was bound by some arcane rule to offer him clemency. Yeah, he had ended things badly, but he gets off with time served because the perception is that the relationship was going to crash anyway. If she acted blindsided, which she truly was, she would be written off as hopelessly naïve. I wish she at least felt she had the option of being hurt and angry. Of believing that what he did more than just sucked.

On the way home from dinner, I wondered why it was on her to "get it." The French have a term, *l'esprit de l'escalier*—the wit of the staircase. It's when you think of the perfect thing to say once you've left a dinner or party. I had that experience in the car, so I don't know what you call it. *L'esprit de l'Escalade,* maybe. Except I wasn't in an Escalade, but the right response did come to me. I can't speak *for* her, but I can correct the way people speak *to* her and *about* her. And about me. A lot of these prophets and prophetesses of doom think they're slick talking under their breath when someone has the audacity to love someone a few years younger. You hear them singing under their breath, rehearsing the runs for their "Cell Block Tango" *Chicago* moment, belting out, "She had it coming! She had it *coming*!"

Nobody has some punishment coming simply for falling in love with another adult. Even the person who changes their mind—as long as the younger person has acted with an appreciation for truth, transparency, and emotional accountability, go in peace. Everyone is free to move the way they need to, and if that's apart, that's fine. But I reject this idea that the younger person isn't accountable for their actions because the older woman is expected to be Miss or Mrs. Congeniality.

I reject that old contract and its "what did you expect?" clause. It was written by people who thought they had a right to calculate my love's worth, and the rate of return on our investment in each other. So, I offer this new contract from the Law Office of Gabrielle Union—for us, by us, we women who have the audacity to age, and hope, and believe in love. The contract isn't for you to sign, it's for the friends and family in our lives who will act as *witnesses* to this love. (Note: if you are getting this secondhand—a dog-eared page on the book given to you, or a clip of audiobook on an Instastory—take a moment and ask if this is meant for you.)

WITNESSETH AS FOLLOWS

WHEREAS, you have been informed that I am in love, and the party is _____ years younger than me; and

WHEREAS, you, my friend, are aware that each of the parties is an adult, we have a separate Agreement with an understanding of mutual trust. We will behave and act in the way we claim to feel; and

WHEREAS, the parties in love understand that each of them has the right to change their mind, to grow at a different rate and speed than each other; and

WHEREAS, I, your friend, know that love is not a guarantee, but heartbreak is not a certainty, either; and

WHEREAS, you, my friend, perhaps think I am giving this person my heart to break, you can disclose this concern of risk but not hold it as an absolute guarantee of outcome.

In consideration of the mutual promises contained herein and with the desire to be legally bound by the provisions of this Agreement, the Parties jointly agree as follows:

1. You, the undersigned, pledge to uphold the Fourteenth Amendment's guarantee of Equal Protection, and recognize that parties forming relationships in different age brackets have been subject to unjustified criticism and inequality in the eyes of friends and family.

2. You hereby acknowledge that it is hard enough for me to find someone to love who won't ruin my credit, and you, my friend, desire to encourage me to be hopeful for an "amazing" outcome.

3. I am aware that "amazing" is not a legal term, and is subject to different definitions. For the purposes of this Arrangement, the Parties agree that it means simply that you allow me to dream.

4. Because your opinion matters to me and I feel better knowing you have my back, if and when my Arrangement dissolves—either in amicable clarity or in an instance of slashed tires—you agree to continue to have said back.

WE, THE UNDERSIGNED PARTIES, have read this Agreement thoroughly. This Agreement expresses our intent and by signing below, we acknowledge our individual desires to be bound by its terms.

Witness Signature _____ Date _____

All I expect, and I would like to think deserve, is for my relationship to be treated with the same hope as any other. Now, if you'll excuse me, I need to find my IcyHot.

9

INTO THE MATRIX

You couldn't just walk in to Extensions Plus expecting vault hair. You had to earn it.

Not just as in the fortune that a good weave cost, but the owner, Helene, had to like you. If she didn't think you worthy of the hair, you weren't getting it.

"I have an audition," I said. She nodded. Every girl in Hollywood had an audition.

"It's for the *Matrix* sequels," I said. "I'm meeting with Joel Silver and the Wachowskis." The movie had made half a billion dollars internationally, but it was the casual drop of the names that got the desired effect. Helene raised her chin just slightly, at the mention of one of the most successful film producers of all time and the famous writer-director siblings. It was early 2002, and those people could name their price in Hollywood.

I was up for the part of Zee, who would be in both sequels. Every Black woman in Hollywood aged twenty to forty-five wanted it. Aaliyah had been cast in the part, but her tragic death in a helicopter crash the previous August meant they needed to recast. I had a vision for Zee, one that went against the expected look of all-black, streamlined trench coats. The character was maternal, but able to operate a bazooka, so I wanted something that was of this earth. Soft, yet powerful.

"I was thinking . . ." I said to Helene, acting like I just happened to have this photo in my purse. I pulled it out and handed it to her. She smiled.

The photo was of Janet Jackson.

Now, if you are as much of a fan as I am, I will pinpoint the Janet moment in the photo. It's from a summer of 1993 shoot, a long-sleeved white gauzy V-neck crop-top sweater and tiny red-tag Levi's with the perfect slouch under her chiseled navel.

And the hair. A cascade of curls swept back from the left to fall down the right side of her face. Yes, the "If" video hair.

I wanted to channel that soft power for Zee. I'd already gotten the working-actress version of the outfit scouring the racks at Contempo Casuals and trying on hundreds of Levi's to find the perfect ones. But to really get the look, I needed Helene to open the special vault of hair. To give me the most pristine whatever-virgin-died-at-some-temple hair.

Helene nodded. I exhaled. I'd passed the test. I held it like a talisman on the way to my car.

For the day of the audition, I lined up Kim Kimble, a hairstylist who would work magic with the weave, and planned to go straight from her salon to the studio. In her chair, with a makeup artist at the ready, I was transformed into my vision.

"Do you want the mole?" the makeup artist asked.

Janet Jackson has a perfect beauty mark on the left side of her face, just above her top lip. I was so caught up in being Janet that I had to go full force. "Yes," I answered.

I walked out of that salon ten times more powerful than when I walked in. I drove differently, a coquettish smile to every red light. *I'll allow it,* I thought. I was, after all, on my way to meet destiny. They would be filming in Australia—it would be a full lockdown on my time, but completely worth it. I turned up my stereo, blaring "The Pleasure Principle." "You might think I'm crazy, but I'm serious," I sang.

I got to the Warners lot, where I had been given drive-on privileges. No street parking for this *Matrix* star. The space I was allotted was right by Joel Silver's production office, which I took as not just an omen, but a nod to our working relationship. I walked right to the door of his office. The door to my blockbuster destiny.

I walked in fifteen minutes before my appointment, giving full Janet realness. The receptionist gave me a funny look, stared at me a second, and seemed flustered. *It's working,* I thought. *She's thinking,* This one isn't like the others. What a look!

I was amped up on my Janet music, completely off-book on my life, and sitting there as confident as hell. Minutes ticked by. I'm early, I thought, it's cool. And really, I was in the zone. I was going to walk in there and Joel Silver and the Wachowski siblings were going to say, "There's our Zee. She is not like anyone we've seen."

When the door into the office opened, I turned to see what sad sucker was going to have to follow me.

And in walked Janet Jackson.

She was there for *her* audition for Zee. The real Janet Jackson, dressed in the *Matrix* garb of black and leather. Janet started to say something to the receptionist, and then her eyes fell on me. She leaned back, speechless, but the look on her face unmistakably said, *What in the creepy fuck?*

I was speechless, too, breaking into an immediate sweat because I had never met her and was such a fan. Now, here I was dressed as a bootleg bargain basement version of her, down to the mole. Except for my weave, which cost a fortune.

"Uhhh," she finally said, but because it was Janet Jackson, they were waiting for her whenever she arrived. Joel Silver and the Wachowskis burst out of the office in excitement. "Hello, Janet," they said in a chorus. "Come this way." They didn't even look at me, but Janet could not take her eyes off me, her gaze turning into a pitying side-eye as she entered the audition room.

All I was missing was a red clown nose. My makeup was sweating off my face, and I would later realize the mole had run into a streak.

When they walked Janet out after her audition, I pretended to be very interested in the hole in the knee of my jeans so I didn't have to look at any of them.

"Wow," one of the Wachowskis said once she was gone. Then they turned to me. There was an odd pause as they took in this sight. "Yeah, come in," said Joel.

It didn't get better from there. I barely remember the actual audition, and what was the point? Why take the dollar-store Janet when you could have the real thing? But neither Janet nor I ended up getting the part. Nona Gaye did. For a while I wondered if we had somehow canceled each other out. Or if Janet now hated me. I pictured her psyching herself up for the audition, listening to whoever *her* idol was. Marching in there to show them Janet the actress. The *star*. In a look she had chosen that said, "I am ready to be Zee."

And there I was, a cosmic joke with a streaky mole, dressed up in my Janet-the-singer cosplay.

———

Two years later, I was partying at Club Bed in Miami after *Bad Boys II* was released. Club Bed was exactly that, a nightclub with beds lining the perimeter, all separated by gauzy curtains in a giant room full of pink and lavender lights. There was the ultra-VIP bed in the center near the dance floor, where you could see everything, and toward the way back, there I was with Wilmer Valderrama and one of his best friends, Tadao Salima, who did security. We were doing our version of popping bottles, but not the best ones. Just the ones the non-leads of *That '70s Show* and *City of Angels* could afford. Balling on a budget.

Wilmer and Tadao returned from a walk around the club. "Yo, Gab," said Wilmer. "Jermaine Dupri just said he wants to introduce you to Janet." Jermaine was dating Janet at the time, and I had known him for a while.

"Now?" I actually said. Here's what I said in my head: "I am sweaty from being in a club all night and this is not the outfit I want her to meet me in because the last time she saw me I was dressed as her and I thought it was weird so I know she thought it was *really* fucking weird."

So, I just refused.

Wilmer and Tadao then proceeded to drag me through the crowded club to her VIP bed in the middle. They brought me to her security, just like parents bringing a kid to the front of the line to meet Santa at a department store.

"Oh, right this way," said one of the guards.

"Really?"

He moved his body so I could see Janet in her large group. Well, the back of her head. The girl she was talking to looked at me, and then leaned forward and whispered something in Janet's ear. In my mind, what I was hearing is "That creepy bitch from the *Matrix* audition is here. She's still fucking sweating and still fucking weird."

Janet popped up and turned, and gave me the most amazing soul hug. And she said, still holding my arms, "I'm so proud of you."

I immediately started bawling like I *was* that kid meeting Santa. She heard it all: "I have loved you since *Diff'rent Strokes*. Charlene. Your hair, Willis Drummond *chose you* . . . *Fame* . . . Oh, God, Cleo on *Fame* . . . " This verbal diarrhea continued, and I will spare you in a way that I did not Janet.

She was grace personified, saying in her light voice, again and again, "I love it. I love it." Like a gentle bird gliding over the mess. "Stay," she finally said. "Hang out." I looked back at Wilmer and Tadao, my proud parents standing there with a thumbs-up. Their little sweaty creeper had made it.

All these years later, she's the friend who reminds me to set my clocks back. We are the older moms in our group, and we just get each other. She's good for a funny meme, or the text that says, "Hey, I just thought of you . . . How are you doing?"

I confess that every time she pops up unexpectedly on my phone, I think of that sweaty creeper. Last year, I finally had to ask her. "Hey, uh, do you remember the *Matrix* audition?"

Her face briefly fell into a look of intense pity, and she touched my knee in consolation. "Oh," she said. "I was not gonna bring that up."

And then she laughed. That perfect Janet laugh.

10

FUCK BALANCE

I'm going to tell you a secret about life. You might know part of it, but chances are you don't know the whole story.

Wait, hold on. You're multitasking right now, aren't you? You can't even read or listen to a book without having something else productive going on. This is exactly the thing I am talking about: whether or not you have kids, there's that creeping sense that you are borrowing your time from others. If it's not your family, it's your job, your friendships, your abs, and the most guilt-inducing, your potential. Anything for you is at the expense of something or someone else, and you're always in the red.

Your life is not just a hamster wheel. It's an elaborate but creaky system of about five wheels you are expected to keep moving with precision timing. *You* know the whole thing is being held together with some gum here, acrylic-nail glue there, and maybe a dried-out but still passably sticky Band-Aid you found in your bag. You tell yourself that if you make one wrong step, the whole thing will fall apart, but the truth is if you make *any* step, the whole contraption is liable to fall down on your hamster ass.

But you keep going, and the second things start to go off track, the helpful message you get is, "Find *balance!*" It's always phrased as something you need to "find," right? As if it's waiting to be discovered and you just haven't tried hard enough.

You won't find it. Because balance doesn't exist.

"Balance" is actually a multilevel marketing program—what we used to call a pyramid scheme. You know those things. They target your high school friend or cousin, usually a woman who has kids, and tell them to invest their money in a product and then sell it to their friends and family. Worse, these women are told to recruit their friends to become "consultants" so they can access their network. I guarantee you, check your old Facebook inbox—there's a message lurking in there that begins "Hey girl!" as a preamble to tell you about an exciting opportunity involving nonessential oils or tie-dye leggings.

No matter how much time or energy they put in, those women never turn a profit. The same goes for balance: you will be continually urged to invest in the idea of balance but never find it as you work yourself to death. Women in the public eye, myself included, are encouraged to promote balance as a concept to everyone in our reach. Whether you're a senator or CEO, an actress or athlete, you need to have a practiced answer for the question every single interviewer will ask you: "How do you find balance?" It doesn't matter how absurd the answer is—"I get up at four A.M. to work out so I can be present as I make breakfast for the kids before work." You just need to have one. Nobody really cares about the answer, mind you, because it doesn't mean a damn thing. It's just about promoting the idea that some equilibrium exists as a *possibility*. A reach. And that if you work hard enough, sacrifice even more of your time or self, you will achieve this feeling. So, go ahead! Overextend yourself. Hustle more, complain less. If you and your friends are not greeting each other with "I'm so tired" then you are doing it wrong.

Deep down, you have known that this is a lie. That nagging suspicion you're being conned is what's leading to that feeling of rage inside you. The current of anger runs under all the emotions that demand your attention: isolation, resentment, self-doubt. But it's the rage that surprises you. There's some tipping point you never see coming that makes your whole day unravel.

You race for an elevator with a bag and a baby, and you just need someone to hold the door. And they don't.

You are managing your family's schedule and ask your husband the most basic question. He sighs, having to think for a moment about what you have to think about all the time.

You have engineered your workday to the minute in order to be off at 5:00, so you can pick up the kids from practice, but your boss tells you at 4:50 that they need you to stay longer to salvage the work some mediocre coworker did a half-ass job on.

Those tipping points put you on the verge of tears and rage. When your anger pops out like that, it feels foreign, it feels powerful, and yet so essentially *you* that it makes everything else about you seem false. It's your primal fight-or-flight response to being trapped. Adrenaline floods your bloodstream, your heart rate increases with your blood pressure, and your prefrontal cortex—the part of your brain that does the smart stuff—shuts down so the faster-acting, primitive parts of the brain can do the work.

But what happens to us when we're always trapped? What do we do with all that adrenaline? All that ragey rage?

I rebelled from the party line in interviews years ago, but not enough. Before Kaavia James was born, reporters asked me how I balance work and "home"—meaning my marriage and life as a stepmother. Dwyane was never asked about this, mind you. I was the only custodian asked to give progress reports. Once Kaav was born, the stakes seemed higher and the questions more pointed. "How do you make it all work?" was the question.

"We just *try* to make it work," I would say, and I would make a point of acknowledging that it was hard, but we also had advantages like paid caregivers. "You do your best."

What I should have said, and what I ask you to say now, is "Fuck balance."

I know for a fact that balance is a lie, because this year I came so close to the mirage, I could almost taste that cool water. It looked so refreshing that I fell to my knees and made cups of my hands to scoop up all the balance. The thing that all these superwomen say keeps them going. Give it *all* to me.

But when I brought it to my lips, it was sand. Believe me, I had every single advantage available to me, and it was still a mirage. The system, you see, is rigged against women.

———

The first five years of marriage with Dwyane were in some ways unconventional. We had very active but separate schedules. I was also a stepmother, so my role in the family had a different set of expectations. But in many ways, it was like most marriages. The male was the breadwinner, and the female generally managed the home. For many years, the life of that home was dictated by my husband Dwyane's schedule and needs. I don't think people have an understanding of what goes into getting an athlete of his age and caliber ready every day. If he had practice at 10 A.M., he was up at 7:30. Quick breakfast and a full workout, before a three-hour practice. Then another workout, shooting drills with another coach. Then maybe he'd come home and have a nap. When he napped, the world stopped. The kids put on headphones, and we had a houseful of people moving around like mice. Then there would be specialists—the cupping person, the masseuses, and the physical therapists arriving to make sure his body was working properly. This was a practice day, not even a game day when he had to travel. And there were no "days off," because a day off from the team just meant he was doing charity work like visiting sick kids for Make-a-Wish, and seeing to business ventures outside his life as an athlete. This didn't leave time for, well, most things. No parent-teacher conferences, or really anything having to do with school. Like many men, he was not much involved in the nuts-and-bolts parenting that happens during business hours.

He played for sixteen years, and had full custody of the kids for nine of them. Here was a father who was interviewed every day—after every single practice and game—and at no point did anyone ever ask him, "How do you manage it all?" Because there was never an expectation that he—or any man—had to. All the balance he needed to bring home was tied to the bank account. As long as he was making money, somebody else was going to do the rest.

Dwyane could have a small army of staff and caregivers—and

me—to make this happen, but there was never once a sense that he had somehow ceded his authority as Dad. He *delegated* his power, while retaining all of it. I mean, allllll of it. He could show up at any point and no one would question that he had final say on any subject.

But women? Moms don't get to "delegate" power without losing something. That is characterized as farming out responsibility and passing on our duties. Prioritizing career over family, and letting someone else raise our kids. The expectation is that I have to work twelve hours a day, go to the kids' games, be on top of their homework, look good, see to meals, nurture the egos around me, handle a house, laundry, birthday parties, groceries, checkups, *and* fuck somebody? What? Yes, because if in all that juggling you drop a ball, it's on you. Whether you lose your job or your husband's interest, your high schooler gets an F or your kid is the mean one on the playground, the buck stops at the mother, doesn't it? "Your priorities are off."

Here's the thing. I was aware that I shared the disparities in power and responsibility that a lot of women do, but they didn't affect my day-to-day. I was a stepmother who consistently traveled for work, coming home for thirty-six hours at a time to do my best to catch up before I had to leave again. I could know the issues existed, but I had the luxury of ignoring them.

Then two things happened: we had a baby, and six months later, Dwyane retired. Last year, he told me he wanted the whole family to be together more. My job—my full-time-plus-extra job—was going to become the primary focus. The plan was to now give me and my work the same support and shared focus he had in the years he was the sun we all revolved around. This was a massive change in prioritizing needs.

"It's you now," he told me, meaning it. I know he believed that.

To do that, we had to move our home base from Miami to Los

Angeles. For me to travel less, and be home more, I needed to be where most of the business of Hollywood happens. We moved across the country, I found schools for the kids and a house, and we put everything in place. Here we were all in the same space, with the two of us to attack all of the things. Now . . . balance!

Annnnnd no.

Dwyane is wonderful, but like most men, he has never *not* been the central adult in a family dynamic. A power struggle ensued, one that has continued after this one-year experiment.

"You need a wife," a girlfriend told me.

"No, I need help from my husband," I said.

Most women's work, whether it happens outside the home or in, is not seen. And if it's seen, it is generally unacknowledged. The saying is "never let 'em see you sweat," but it's really about keeping all effort invisible. And how can we expect a family to respect work that they do not see? My work is mainly solitary. Whether I am writing or reviewing a script for production or acting, I go off somewhere. If I were to read a script in the living room, it would be purely for performance in the moment—something out of *Soapdish*. Like Sally Field's character making herself the center of attention to show the work of a *thespian*. Not only do they not see the effort of the work, their understanding of my job is that it takes me away from them. They see absence, and for a mom figure at least, that absence can feel like neglect. But when they talk about their friends' parents who are forever present, they say, "Oh my God, her mom is so annoying. She is all in our business." Well, yeah, because her kids are her job. So, which do you want? Do you really want a mom who's always around and knows all the tea and all the flavors of Kool-Aid? Or a mom with her own life who models power and success for you, but maybe can't make you brownies?

I was stuck trying to be both, doing just enough of both roles to not feel like a failure. Even with all my advantages, I remember one day trying to manage my work schedule with childcare for Kaavia James, interviewing a new tutor for one of the boys, and making room for another extracurricular for Zaya. As I was figuring this all out, I realized I was about to be late for a Zoom call about a show I'm producing.

I was searching for the link when I saw Dwyane pass by. "Babe, can you hand me a water?" I asked, not looking at him.

"I don't work for you," Dwyane said, slow and cool.

He said this to show he was annoyed by "my needs." Whenever he has said something like this, I think of the years I did so many things for Dwyane without being asked. I didn't "work for" him in the sense that I looked at myself as his assistant or employee. I did these things because I saw that he needed something and I could provide it. Anticipated these needs, even. But when I asked for something . . .

I sat there, drowning and overwhelmed, and I felt the rage of my fight-or-flight bubble up. My impulse in the past had been to silence it by silencing myself—because if I opened my mouth, the meanest, most hurtful words might fly out from the worst place of my soul. Something I would never be able to take back.

I didn't want to be the one to kick and scream, "It's my turn!" But, Jesus, it was my turn. All those years we shape-shifted every day to make sure that D had everything that he needed from us did not mean the same would be true for me. While my expectations had apparently gone through the roof, society still had zero expectations of him.

So, here's what I did: I got up and got the water myself. I was a couple of minutes late for the Zoom. I told my team that I was juggling a lot and those couple of minutes were needed.

"I am trying my best," I said, "and I know you all are, too. But sometimes, we don't have it in us to try our best, and we're going to have to hope we have enough decent human beings around us that are also in the same boat."

I would like to tell you that Dwyane and I fixed this immediately after my Zoom meeting. That I called a family meeting and we figured out a perfect 50–50 arrangement. But I know that's never going to happen. I don't want to manage the tit-for-tat of fairness. I want to be able to recognize myself and the bigger picture. I am tired of picking marital fights that don't get us from A to B. I want to be someone who doesn't sweat that somebody's not prewashing the dishes before they stick them in the dishwasher. Is it worth World War III because I do things differently? I don't want to be that person, and I don't have *time* to be that person.

So, I was honest with Dwyane. "In this world we've created in L.A., I need your help," I said. "And sometimes that help is big things. Like moving across the country. And sometimes it's getting me a water. I just need . . ."

I paused a long time. The word swam up from somewhere deep.

"Grace," I said. "I need grace."

Grace, it turns out, is more doable than balance. It's a renewable resource that Dwyane and I can give each other when one of us is in need. Grace, that combination of love and mercy that we all have to give and yet are trained to think we don't deserve.

"I don't have it today." That's all you've got to say. "Got it," is the response.

That's as close to balance as I have found. We find someone, or surround ourselves with people, who we can call upon to pick up our slack. We pick up each other's slack, knowing we will need that same grace soon.

11

DANCE BATTLE

I have never been a fan of Chateau Marmont. Its Gothic architecture looms over Sunset, and a lot of people go in there singing "Hotel California" to themselves, hoping for a residual contact high from its famous inhabitants. No offense, but there is something creepy about the energy. I feel the ghosts of white troubled Hollywood lurking about, turning to look at me like, "And you are?"

But I knew the party there that night was going to be great, and the only thing I like more than a good time is showing a friend a good time. And mine needed it. Let's call her Jenae, and just say up front that her husband was new to playing with the Miami Heat, and I could tell she was getting lost in the size-15 footsteps of the players' fame. This was February 2012, when Dwyane's team was nicknamed the Heatles because they sold out every stadium they toured on the road, just like the Beatles. They were the biggest things in pop culture—even Barack Obama fan-girled out about them. When grown men give up all pretense of cool around your husband, it's easy to get lost in the sauce. I wanted to show her a girls' night out away from Miami.

"I know that you think the guys provide this life alone, but I have had this life for a long time," I told her. "Let me take you out so you can see how this shit can work. Where we're not just the plus-ones, we're the fucking show."

"Okaaay," Jenae said, sounding not in the least bit convinced this was possible.

"Trust me," I said. It was Grammy weekend, and I'd been invited to the Warner Bros. party at Chateau. Since the start of my career, people in the music industry have accepted me and gone out of their way to show me they want me at their parties. I think they just know I am a legit fan, because there's certainly nothing I can do for them. I have no tracks, I'm not producing anything, and the only time anyone ever offered to pay me to sing was a night out with my best friend and hairstylist Larry at a karaoke bar in Woodland Hills. It was the kind of place older, grizzled singers who had a record deal in '78 come in wearing the outfit that got them the deal in '78. Larry and I did our go-to, the Captain and Tennille's "Love Will Keep Us Together," and a booker for a Palm Desert resort ambled over to us.

"You're a pretty thing," he said to me, handing Larry his card. "Do you have booking information?"

I politely said no, and he asked where we usually perform.

"Um, the hair and makeup trailer?" Larry said.

I still have his card somewhere, but he's still the only person who's ever offered me money to sing. I love to, I'm just not good at it by any music industry standard. And yet, for some reason, artists and executives from that world have welcomed me and shown me a kindness that I have not seen at other Hollywood parties. The parties where I was told to arrive late, after the dinner. Black women were supposed to come expecting nothing more than the fact that they were invited; they certainly shouldn't expect to be served food. Or even a seat.

So, all that to say, I felt safe bringing my friend to the party, a girls' night for about eight of us. In the car over, there were Jenae, my friend Aly, the actress A. J. Johnson, and me. We'd gone all out, dressed to impress in sequins and sparkles, beat for the cheap seats. Jenae was talking about how this was the first night she'd really bothered to get really dressed up in a while, since she'd felt invisible at all the basketball events.

"Have you had the thing happen with the valets?" I asked her.

"Where they start to drive off with you—"

"Still in the car!" I finished for her.

"You, too?" she said, grabbing my arm. She thought it was just her.

"Oh, but yes, the valets get so hypnotized seeing Dwyane that I am still in the passenger seat waiting to be let out. We don't exist."

A.J. shot us a look. "Seriously?"

"Seriously," we both said.

But the party was exactly what we needed. We sailed into VIP and the bottles were popping as my friend Serena Williams came over to us for a hug. Serena may be the world's greatest athlete, but to us she is just the world's best karaoke partner. My Palm Desert guy would book her in a second. I kept stealing glances at Jenae, and I could see her having fun. She was blooming in this light. So was I. The ghosts that usually bugged me at Chateau took the night off, maybe seeing the diversity of the crowd and the exuberance of Black energy. I was sipping champagne when we heard it—amazing music coming from inside. We didn't even discuss it, just got up and barreled into the room with everyone else.

It was Bruno Mars, who was only just becoming the Bruno Mars we now know him to be. Today, he is not gonna be the talent at the Warners Grammy office party, but even then, he was a star. He had a full band, flying through songs with electric speed and energy and swag. They performed on a raised stage, the room lit in purple. Of course, we didn't know that Bruno had been part of a wedding band for years, a band that knew how to play *everything*. They were so tight in their camaraderie, playing to each person's strength and moving seamlessly from Michael's "Dirty Diana" to Big Sean's "Dance" and then throwing in Rick James out of nowhere. People put their phones up, and then dropped them just to dance. Around me were John Legend, Reba McEntire, Paul McCartney, Kelly Clarkson, Elvis Costello—like a greatest hits tour of legends. They were all beaming, shaking their heads in wonder because they knew exactly what kind of magic was happening in front of us. These veterans, and us music civilians, recognized a shift in the room and with it the energy of the whole industry.

By the end of that performance, we were all on a high and the liquor was flowing. Those troubled ghosts had been exorcised, at least for that night, and Chateau was ours. We moved to the dance floor, so full of energy we had to release it somewhere, and we Took. It. Over. People naturally gravitated around us, forming a circle just to be near us. I don't know if we ever felt more like stars. This, it must be said, is not how this town usually wants you to feel as Black people. If you feel like a star in Hollywood, you might demand your worth. You might want to be treated like white people. When had

Black women dared be centered? But there we were, at the center of the dance floor. The big prom scene in the movie that had never been written for us.

The DJ created an epic soundtrack for us, every song leading us to grab each other to scream, "This is my jam!" or "That's *my* song!" He reached back into our childhoods, taking something like Jermaine Stewart's "We Don't Have to Take Our Clothes Off," and giving it a new sound so we could *perform* it, not just dance along. The crowd around us got thicker, surrounding us as we were giving and serving *all* of the life force.

It was as Jermaine sang about cherry wine that the crowd suddenly parted to make way for a group of men. I looked up to see a wall of five or six Black guys, smiling at us as they moved toward us in rhythm with the music. Like a schoolyard fight in the best possible way, these guys wanted a dance battle. The crowd started yelling in singsong, "Oh shit! Oh shit!"

I clapped my hands in the air, once, signaling that we accepted the challenge of the dance-off.

Then, fighting to get around somebody at the front, came this whirling five-foot-five dervish of hair and soul. When I say this little motherfucker was the sexiest person at the party? Believe it. Now, we're obviously partnered with some of the biggest athletes in the world, well over six feet, bodies of Adonis, tens of thousands of people screaming for them, every night. But none could compare to the sex appeal of Bruno Mars, Mighty Mousing his way through to stand before us.

Oh shit, I thought. *I just took on the best band in the whole world.*

Bruno nodded at me, leader to leader, even if I was just the de facto one for being foolish enough to accept. But I believed in my girls. I looked back, and Serena's sly smile gave me confidence.

Whitney's "I Wanna Dance with Somebody" came on, and Bruno started easy with some nice moves, lulling me into a sense of security that he was of this earth. The beat dropped and his feet moved so fast, spinning around like an egg beater, as the guys around him hyped the crowd. He dipped to the ground in a split, and came up to this complete moonwalk that made the crowd *lose it.*

He winked at me, like, *What you got?*

I couldn't compete with that, but the sexy grown woman kicked in for me. *I've been here a lot longer than you motherfuckers,* my moves said, dropping it and springing up, giving you the full operation. I whipped my head around, using my weave as an accessory to murder on the dance floor. But I think what sold it, what covered any brief misstep, was the genuine smile stretched across my face.

Reader, I held my own.

Bruno tagged in another dancer, a superflexible long-limbed gymnast incorporating dance tumbling to impress the crowd. I looked at my squad. Aly, who we all affectionately call Tia Aly, locked eyes with me. I nodded, a general in the battle. "Get him."

Aly came up as a dancer, and has this move we all called "Wider" because that's what we chanted whenever she did it. She got in a squat and moved her feet apart farther and farther as she arched her back to do a pop and drop. It was twerking before there was twerking, and it killed with the Chateau crowd, who'd probably never seen anything like that.

Bruno threw up his hands, still in a draw, and his next dancer came in break-dancing to "It's Tricky" and I panicked. *We don't have a break-dancer,* I thought. But Serena was champing at the bit.

"Tag me in! Tag me in!" When the most decorated athlete in the world says she can do something, trust her to deliver.

And Serena Williams proceeded, as the crowd chanted her name, to break it the fuck down. Some rando screamed, "What can't she do?" They were right, but if you have spent an evening hanging with Serena and her sister Venus, music becomes the focal point. Name any city, and she will know some basement club to take you to that takes karaoke dead serious.

Serena was springing up and kicking, and the crowd went wild. Now the whole entire party had closed in around us. It was hot like a basement party in the Bronx.

When the DJ segued into Full Force's "Ain't My Type of Hype," we knew he must have spotted our secret weapon: A. J. Johnson. A.J. was in Kid 'n Play's *House Party,* and her iconic dance battle scene gave "the dance-off" the importance that it has in pop culture. To this day, people re-create her moves at weddings and parties.

"Go, go, go!" I yelled and she was in, doing her signature knee lifts, elbows out. Even if this crowd couldn't tell Kid from Play, they were shocked by the out-of-nowhere precision of her moves. This was a *moment,* and all these people might be here to witness it, but this DJ was playing this music for *us.*

"Beat that," I yelled. But then the whole band and Bruno did the moves right back to her! They could mirror her and add in Kid 'n Play's parts. I raised a fist and yelled, "Foiled!"

As the song ended, Rufus and Chaka's "Ain't Nobody" came on, and I saw Jenae's hand hit the air. I reached out to grab it. "Your turn," I told her. Bruno's crew stepped back as Jenae took the floor. It felt transcendent, watching her have her moment, with even the crew cheering her on. As Chaka says, "Now we're flyin' through the stars, I hope this night will last forever." She was seen, not in reflected glory, but in her own light.

We continued this way—through Guy's "Groove Me" and Janet's "What Have You Done for Me Lately"—until finally we were back to me and Bruno, nose to nose and dripping sweat. This match of my joy and his incredible talent.

With my eyes, I told Bruno, *I respect you, but I am trying to take this crown tonight. I need the fucking win.*

And his eyes said, *Bitch, right back at you. On this night, my night, I want the fucking win.*

We kept battling, and what finally won that night was exhaustion. Exhaustion and mutual respect. Bruno and I hugged like prizefighters trying to stay up, and raised each other's hands in a shared victory. The crowd cheered for both of us.

There was no need to declare a winner because we'd all become friends on the dance floor. Our crew was theirs, and their crew was ours. Everyone in that room knew they were going to be one of the biggest bands in the world, and Bruno one of the brightest stars.

It has to be said: when it gets to the late hour, when it's time to couple up, that's when Black women go out of style. But this crew said *these* women, right here, are the baddest, dopest prizes in here. Bruno offered to share the space, in an equal way, with Black women, and that means seeing us shine. Not "allowing" it—witnessing it. In the dance battle, the feeling was *I see you, I celebrate you, and I challenge you to be even greater.* The joy of connection in spirit that happens when you welcome in Black women—and don't relegate us to holding up the wall—that joy will change your life. It can change the trajectory of a country. We can literally do anything.

Strangers hugged us—real hugs, not Hollywood elbow-clutch hugs—or gave us high-fives as we left to pile into our SUV. We weren't even on the road before we were recounting key moments. "And you . . . *you* with that move! Where the hell did you learn that?"

There are moments you miss out on because you think, *I could stay home. All parties are the same.* No. No, they're fucking not. Because if you missed *this* party, you missed it.

Then there was a stillness in the car, all of us just breathing.

"We were exalted," I said. "Exalted."

We. I had been so intent on helping Jenae step out from her husband's shadow. But the reason I knew what that felt like was because I was right there with her, standing by a six-foot-something Heatle blocking out the sun. Physician, heal thyself.

I had out my hand for Jenae to high-five. The men in our lives didn't make us amazing, or valid; we are rock stars because we are Black women who survived and thrived in the world. And that night, some people recognized that. Even if they hadn't, we could hold each other in regard. Tag ourselves in when we need to shine.

The next morning, I would feel every move I'd made, like I'd done Leg Day for a week. My neck would hurt so much from that heavy hair tossing, I'd be convinced my weave gave me whiplash.

But for that night, we were golden.

12

POWER IN NUMBERS

A girlfriend texted a distress call. For the last year, she had been talking about putting together a film. She did this with such regularity that in the group chat one of us usually just asked, "How's your movie?" because it was all she wanted to talk about anyway.

There was always an update: bringing in another major player, asking what we thought of ideas for casting actors. She was considering big names, and they came in because of her reputation and her enthusiasm for the project. My friend saw that each got their deal done for the film, as she waited to get hers done at the end. She figured she'd get all the ducks in a row first, and then she'd get herself paid. But when it came time to get her deal done, the powers that be tried to offer her way less than one of the newcomers hired to play a supporting role.

"Wait, hold on," she said. "I brought her on. This is my thing. How am I getting fucked?"

At first, they said she should take less if she believed in the project. Wasn't seeing her passion project realized more important to her than a paycheck? She was not born yesterday, so she dismissed that argument.

Ah, but then they said it was exactly because she was *not* born yesterday that they *had* to offer her less. She was older, they said, not some young whippersnapper. It should be understood that she was lucky to work. Never mind that she had an actual track record of opening movies, while the person getting more money had never opened a single one. But this is, of course, bigger than roles or track record. Women are taught to devalue themselves as they age. An accumulation of years, of real experience, triggers some economic law of diminishing returns. Why invest in us?

"Nope," my girlfriend said. "I know what I'm worth. I'm gonna go ahead and pass."

She walked away from this dream project she nurtured into existence. And the first thing she did was let me, and the other girlfriends who would be next on their casting list, know what was up.

"What *is* your worth on this?" I asked. "If they hit me, which you know they will, what's the amount that you feel you should have?"

She gave me that number.

"Bet," I wrote back.

So, of course, here they came. "We've got this great opportunity," they said. They went all through the stars and moon that my friend had hung for this project, not mentioning her once. "You would be perfect for this role. You are exactly who we envision. A Gabrielle Union. *The* Gabrielle Union."

"Yeah, okay," I said. "This is what I need." I gave my friend's number.

They were speechless. Then they offered me even *less* than what they said they would pay her. Hundreds of thousands of dollars less.

So, now I was pissed.

"Well, first off, this is my friend's movie," I said. "What happened there?"

"Oh," they said, seeming surprised that Black women in the industry talk to each other, let alone about money. "We couldn't make a deal."

"Oh," I said, matching their cadence. "Why couldn't you make a deal?"

They came up with some nonsensical reason, vague and diaphanous. Chiffon draped over bullshit. I just wanted to know how diabolical they would be in coming up with half-truths, since I knew the real reason. Hollywood deals are like sex. People will lie "I love you" to get the deal done.

I passed, and immediately texted my girlfriend to tell her. "I was who they envisioned. LOL."

We agreed on who would be the next call on the list. And then the person after that, and the person after that. We were right every time. Mind you, the number they offered got lower and lower as they went down the list, but our self-worth did not. We each asked for the same price, banding together in solidarity to *not* present them with the cheaper option. To not be the person used to screw over somebody that is deserving of what they're asking for.

The longer it took, the more they risked losing the other girl, the actress who had gotten the bigger check. Finally, when the younger ingenue realized my girlfriend was out, she said, "I'm not gonna do this without the person that brought me to the dance."

They had to step up, and they ended up paying my friend more than what she initially asked for. Sometimes using your position of privilege isn't to ensure your paycheck, it's to ensure the next person's paycheck. And to make sure they are treated with the respect and dignity that they deserve. You have that power if you choose to use that power. That's why it's so important that women talk about what we make and be open about our experiences in the workplace. Knowing what other people make and *why* is not only about doing better for yourself, but to make sure that people who are really doing the work and putting in the extra effort are being rewarded, and not just used as mules.

And maybe, for a lot of us on that list, it was practice. Getting over our fear of being perceived as the uppity Negro or the person that asks for their actual worth as opposed to being fine with crumbs as long as they keep coming. At what point do you get to that space of taking a chance on yourself?

The reality is it's only been relatively recently that I've come to this understanding. It's hard to admit that for a very long time, I didn't really understand my value at all, not in a financial sense or even on a spiritual or emotional level. I had to ask myself what I ask you now: What's your worth versus what you take? And why?

Sometimes the why is a ratio of fear and need, and I get that. When you're head of a household, you don't always feel like you're in a position to bet on yourself. You know that anything can happen, so you take what you're offered without any negotiation. There have been times in my career—fine, many times—where I took an opportunity out of a fear of never working again. When I was just getting started I would see people who used to be famous. The girl group member working the register at Target. The onetime sitcom regular taking my order at California Pizza Kitchen. The former sitcom star wearing the same sweats to the dog park every day. Each was a terrifying memento mori: "What you are, I was; what I am, you will be."

When I started really moving around Hollywood, and working consistently, I wondered why people didn't plan for the "never again." I lived in terror that I wouldn't know when the "never again" was coming until the phone stopped ringing. "Last call, already?"

But what happens when you *only* think of that? How do you rob yourself of really reaping the benefits of everything you bring to the table, the piles of cash and time you gave a company, or even a family? Because even when dealing with people you are friendly with, there can be a refusal to share the wealth. The people who wave and blow kisses to you while you're in the trenches will claim your victory and take the spoils of your success as theirs. You're playing a part in building their wealth or the profits of a company; they are at the dance and don't want to pay the person who got them there. They want to profit from an economy, as a Black female producer I know once told me, "that was not built for us, but was built by us."

Certainly, a lot of people prey on the most marginalized. They take advantage of the fact that Black and brown people often have not had the resources of therapy and also are working in spaces where very few people look like them. Treated like the magical Negro—or magical marginalized—they might choose to make you a face of the company without giving you the support needed. Post a photo of you on their socials and hashtag it #blackgirlmagic. It's a proven profit-winner: use your narrative for PR or to check a box, and then exploit the inevitable impostor syndrome that results. Because we know it's not magic, it's work. And we will work three times as hard to live up to the expectation that hashtag brings, not just because we were raised knowing the lengths we will have to go in order to be taken seriously professionally, but also because there's usually somebody who's willing to step in right behind you and take less. Or gladly be abused and have their "magic" used.

My friend was supposed to accept crumbs, because they already had that list in mind of others they thought would gladly take her spot for even less. But once you know your value you won't want to be complicit in that. Success will naturally have to look different for you then, but if we give ourselves time away from the fear that's been instilled in us, we have space to decide what our true success really is.

For me, success is now about change. I need to be able to look around at others so I can be sure everyone has something to eat on their plate. It's no longer enough to just stare down at my own tray, so overflowing with "abundance" that I'm never going to even have a chance to eat. It used to be, but that shit don't taste good anymore. I lost my appetite.

13

THANKSGIVING

"It's amazing, right?"

My mother didn't answer me, just leaned in closer to examine the oil painting in my friend's foyer. I'd asked her to stop by my friend Kyle's house, but this tour of his home was the real reason I had invited her. I knew my mother, the woman who'd taken me to so many museums as a kid, would love his art collection.

It was just the two of us, with Kyle outside hosting a barbecue for all of his friends in the seventy-degree weather of late-November Arizona. This was the Wednesday before Thanksgiving 2008, and my mom and I were both visiting Phoenix. When Kyle first greeted her, he apologized for the chill, but in my mother's Omaha the day had started ten degrees below freezing.

I was in town from L.A. to spend the holiday with my father, who had moved to the area after divorcing my mother fifteen years before. My little sister Tracy had moved to be near him, and my mother was doing what many divorced parents of adult children do: seizing an unobtrusive opportunity to see their kids together. My parents were still not in a place where they could share a holiday, though that would come. For now, we still divvied up our calendars according to who had called dibs years before. My father and my stepmother, who love gatherings, chose Thanksgiving. By the time I sat to eat turkey the next day, my mother would be back to her life and family in Omaha, but this Wednesday belonged to us.

We continued through the quiet mansion, and every turn revealed more of the collection. It was mostly religious iconography—tempera and gold representations of Jesus next to huge oil paintings of saints in biblical settings. Kyle shared my mother's deep love and appreciation for Catholic art, and was able to afford this house and everything in it because of his previous career in adult entertainment. It's not something he disavowed, it's just that he's a businessman and that was an early venture.

This private show of the work was sort of my gift to her out here in this dry, flat landscape my father had claimed, an unexpected desert outpost of the culture and faith she loves. She visited with the paintings like friends, murmuring the names of the saints depicted. "Saint Dominic," she said. "Oh, the Nativity of Mary. How nice."

"How do you know that baby is Mary?" I asked.

She leaned in closer. "Well, that's Saint Anne holding her." She paused when I said nothing. "Her *mother*. And there's usually a bit of blue in the painting. Mary's color."

Kyle and my mom were two Catholic kids who grew up going

to Mass. These were family photos to them. I knew he had religious artifacts and relics in his trophy room, so I led her there.

"Oh my gosh," she said. There were shelves of awards, plus signed sports memorabilia under glass. So much so that she might have assumed Kyle was an athlete. "Well, whatever he does, he's got to be really good at it. He's got a lot of trophies."

"Yeah," I said, as she leaned in to read the inscription at the bottom of one large crystal trophy. I saw her eyes widen, and she turned to look at me.

I read it silently over her shoulder. "Best Couples Sex Scene."

"Oh," I said, offhand. "Kyle was a porn titan."

"Well," she said. "I like his taste in art, and I'm glad he does well for himself." She continued to look at the art, no judgment in her voice as she said quietly, "All your friends always do so well for themselves."

———

If my mother raised me to not judge people, my father and I are similar in that we are gatherers of people. If he is hosting, it's come one, come all. He encouraged me to bring as many people as possible to Thanksgiving at his home, so of course I invited Kyle and all of his friends. In addition to a few girlfriends, I also invited a crew of guys from Lafayette, Louisiana, my girlfriends and I had met one night hanging in Las Vegas. Like I said, I am a collector of people.

I'd also invited my newish boyfriend, Dwyane, who was in town to play against the Phoenix Suns and do a paid club appearance Thanksgiving night. Did I mention that he was flying his mother Mama Wade and his older sister Tragil from Chicago to come, too? Mama Wade is a formidable figure, having turned her life around from being an absentee mother dealing with drug addiction, to becoming a pastor.

Come one, come all.

On Thanksgiving Day, my job was to bring the alcohol. My stepmother spends days, if not weeks, preparing and cooking for Thanksgiving, so her kitchen was her fiefdom. But booze I could do.

So, picture Dwyane Wade, a former porn titan, and all of his friends and me in Safeway at noon on Thanksgiving Day. We had to be at my dad's by one o'clock. Black people eat Thanksgiving dinner mad early.

This was when Dwyane was Sober Sally, so he was noncommittal on what we should get. He was in his mid-twenties, still figuring out his relationship with alcohol after growing up surrounded by addiction and its consequences. He looked at drinking as a risk that led to being out of control, and when we were out in Miami he saw me as a walking PSA for sober living. After a few drinks I would cuss out his friends for their freeloading, and he used to say he needed to curb my drinking "for your own good" when it was really to spare his friends' feelings.

"When you're out with me, you get two drinks, max," he said at the beginning of one night. So "Two Drinks Max" became my nickname for Dwyane among my girlfriends, who would sneak me drinks under the table.

Our shopping cart was full of wine, beer, tequila, Hennessey, vodka—a smorgasbord of drunkenness—but I thought we still needed something festive. "What would be good?" I said aloud, twirling slightly to scan the store. And like a beacon of yellow, there it was: a display of limoncello, bright and inviting. So harmless in its lemony vibrancy.

"Yo, did you see Danny DeVito on *The View*?" I asked everyone.

DeVito had admitted on the air that he was still drunk from a night of limoncello with George Clooney. The dopey smile of Danny, with the class of Clooney—isn't that what we all want in a buzz?

Somebody offered: "Yeah, I heard that if you, like, freeze it, it's like a lemonade slushy."

"Sold!" I yelled, grabbing bottles. Two Drinks Max sighed. I headed to the checkout, then circled back to grab two more. "Can't afford not to," I said. "Best to err on the side of caution." The first and last time that caution meant getting *more* booze. "We're having a party."

When we got to my dad's house, we immediately put the limoncello in the large freezer to slush up, then set up two bar stations, one by the kitchen and one outside near the gazebo. This was Dwyane and my dad's first holiday together, and things were still a little awkward from their last meeting. That one had ended with my father asking Dwyane out of nowhere if he was after my money. "Dad, save me from the millionaire who wants my thousands!" Meanwhile, the Lafayette crew took to my dad like white on rice and he treated them like long-lost nephews. Kyle and his crew worked their polite charms, and we were off to the races.

"Where's Chris?" I asked my sister Tracy, though I knew. At these events, my stepmother Chris would cook and cook for days, then become overwhelmed early and retreat to her room. Guests were then expected to make their way upstairs and stand in a receiving line. At the time, I didn't understand that it probably was overwhelming to have that many people in her home.

My dad constantly asked me, "Have you gone up to see her yet?"

I played dumb. "No, I figured she'd be down. Since there's a houseful of people? Is she sick?"

With the hostess upstairs, Thanksgiving didn't have much of a game plan. That was fine, though, as we just started playing spades and drinking the booze. It became a real party, and my dad and I caught each other looking around the room at the same time, pleased with ourselves for bringing so many people together. There was his own collection of stray foundlings, plus my stepmother's family, all having a blast with the crews I brought: Dwyane's Chicago faction, the Cajun guys from Lafayette, and the porn empire.

The food was laid out on the table, and Dad had us put the extra leaf in just to hold it all. As usual, we gathered to say grace around the table, all these onetime strangers holding hands in a circle. We had two pastors present, Mama Wade and Chris's brother, so there was an awkward moment where we had to figure out who should say grace. "Do rock paper scissors," someone suggested, but Mama Wade immediately bowed out. In my stepmother's absence from hosting, her brother would assume grace duties.

He proceeded to launch into the *Iliad* of graces. This kindly man did a whole-ass performance, with twists and turns, shouts and singing. Those moments when you thought it was finally over? He was just taking a breath before continuing his audition for *America's Next Top Preacher*. At that point, most of the guests were at least tipsy, and some were drunk. So, we were peeking at each other and starting to giggle as we squeezed each other's hands. By the end someone let loose with a full-on snicker, which started a lot of us chuckling, and suppressing it left us shaking in a crying laughter. I caught Mama Wade opening her eyes to give a disapproving look. She did not know what to make of this laughing through grace. Dwyane, stone-cold sober, bit his lip.

Finally, we all took plates to the tables set up around the house. There were so many people that new friends grabbed spots together on couches and the stairs. I noticed Tracy acting . . . well, anyone who has a younger sister will understand this: she was acting very "little sister." She clearly wanted to peacock a little but wasn't sure how exactly to get in there. She was still young for her age, even in her mid-twenties. That stage where you want to entertain and *be* entertained.

So, she kept drinking.

Almost as soon as the meal was over, people began wrapping the leftovers. My stepmother still had not come down, so people put the food away wherever they saw room. A thrilled "What's *this?!*" rang out from the kitchen.

This was the limoncello in the freezer, now slushy and ready to pour. We were already so drunk, we began pouring the bright yellow liqueur into tumblers and chanting, "Limoncell-*ohhh.*"

Again, it's a liqueur, meant to be sampled in dainty doses. And it was insta-crack. We were all on Ten immediately. Like the alcohol gods had snapped their fingers on Mount Olympus and said, "Let's watch them get *really* fucked up."

Dwyane and I sat to play spades, teaming against my dad and my friend Ryan, one of the Lafayette boys. We were trash-talking cash shit. My dad and Dwyane were getting along, and I remember thinking, as the music blared and people danced behind me, *This is the best Thanksgiving ever.*

Then I heard the opening call and response of Beyoncé's "Single Ladies" and smiled broader. As we kept playing spades, I saw my dad look up toward the kitchen behind me, where most of the people were dancing. He returned his gaze to his cards, which he held in an increasingly tight death grip, then back to whatever was happening behind me. He looked down, pursing his lips and doing a slow, exaggerated head shake.

What is he . . . I thought, turning to look behind me. I gasped. *Oh.*

My little sister Tracy was doing the "Single Ladies" dance, and she was *nailing* it. Beyoncé would have given her the floor. Tracy was twisting her hips, going forward low, then back. There was just one issue: Beyoncé did all that in a leotard, but Tracy was wearing a shirt with a plunging neckline. Actually, it wasn't even so plunging, it's just that Tracy has large breasts. The boobs were kind of everywhere.

People gathered around to cheer her on, and I would say for sure that people were honestly just marveling that this little sister had the choreography *down*. But my dad just saw everyone watching his daughter dancing in a way that he felt was too suggestive. The Lafayette boys, the porn titan friends, his friends, and not one but *two* pastors.

A chant began of "Go Tracy! Go Tracy!" Friends egging her on as she dipped lower, stuck her butt out more, flipped her hand back and forth looking for a ring. She was a spectacle. Her peacock moment had arrived. She *loved* it.

After one last gyration, my dad threw his hand of cards down, pushed his chair back, and stomped over to her where she was bending low.

"GET UP!" he yelled, grabbing her by the arm. Tracy was furious, her moment stolen. He took her outside to the front of the house to reprimand her, talking to her like she was eight years old. And you could hear her responding in kind. *"Da-ad."*

We couldn't *not* watch, because now it was a movie on the big screen of the bay window. And everyone heard my little sister scream. "You don't know me, Dad! *You don't fucking know me!*"

It was shocking to me, because we are not the type of family that cusses in front of our parents, and definitely not *at* our parents. That's some white-folks stuff, and in that moment, Tracy was basically Jon Snow battling the White Walkers. Even the porn guys were like, *Whoa*.

"What *doesn't* he know?" someone from Lafayette said, drunk logic making him curious.

"What don't *we* know?" said one of the porn boys, as if it was a deep, existential question. Everyone looked at each other and nodded, stoned on limoncello. Tracy stormed off from our dad and half-heartedly headed to the cars, knowing we would stop her.

We had a cab bring her home with a girlfriend and Thanksgiving was abruptly over. We had flown too close to the bright sun of limoncello. My dad came in to say "turn off that music" before going upstairs. I pictured him trying to piece together the afternoon for my stepmother, who now really had something to take to the fainting couch about. With the parents upstairs, there was a sense that we were all teenagers who'd been busted.

Dwyane had to do his Thanksgiving night appearance, and we all felt so grounded by my dad that a bunch of us leaving for that felt like a prison break. At the club, Dwyane reverted to Two Drink Max, keeping an eye on me. But I'd hit my limit anyway. Toward the end of the night, my sister Tracy appeared at the club like a ghost of Thanksgiving past. She'd gone home and went right to sleep. Had she puked and rallied?

"Hi, Beyoncé," I said.

She looked at me, puzzled.

I laughed. "You don't remember, do you?" I said, launching into a quick recap of the dance-a-thon.

"I did that?" she said. "Well, it's not a big deal."

"It kind of was," I said, putting an arm around her. "It ended Thanksgiving. But hey, you were great."

"I was?" Under the lights of the club, I looked at my little sister, the one who had tried so hard to find her place in a room full of big personalities. She is different than me and my dad. My father and I live in our heads so much that when we decide to go hard, we need to fill the space around us with people and drinks. We fill the room so we *don't* feel like we stand out as different. But she wanted her moment.

"Yes," I said. "You were amazing."

I wanted to give my sister that gift of grace and admiration, the same way I offered my mother the unexpected opportunity to admire the blue in a painting of Mary, or my father a houseful of guests to host so he could feel that pride. Maybe part of adulthood is learning how to be as kind to family as we are to friends.

Any bad feelings from my father about the day didn't last. Even all these years later, my friends have a standing invite to Thanksgiving at my dad's. Especially the Lafayette boys, who adopted my Omaha-born dad into their Louisiana family. Kyle is married and has his own family now, one to mesh with his chosen family of friends.

In Union family lore, I have always described this as "the time limoncello ruined Thanksgiving." And it's true that it ended abruptly on a negative note. The upside is that it proved my family, as fractured as it had been, was just like anyone else's: we have squabbles and misunderstandings at Thanksgiving and we get over it.

I know Tolstoy said, "All happy families are alike; every unhappy family is unhappy in its own way," but to me, periods of unhappiness are something that all families have in common. There are unavoidable battles, with each other and within ourselves. We all fight our dragons, and if you are lucky—or simply intentional—your family is committed to slaying those dragons together. One limoncello at a time.

Just not too many.

14

THE GOLDEN LADY OF L.A.

The essay you are reading now is a time capsule, one I'm starting near the beginning of the COVID-19 quarantine in L.A. As the author, I know I'm supposed to be the one leading the conversation, but as I write this, I feel like you're way ahead of me in time and I'm afraid to ask how we did.

As I write this, we are a few weeks into lockdown, and I have found myself sleeping later and going to bed earlier. A thread of days fell away until they were in a pile. The other morning, I was awakened by the sound of Kaavia James laughing. She usually wakes up around seven or eight, and normally I get right in there. When she wakes up in her crib already laughing at something from a dream or some conversation in her head, it's the best stand-up routine you can see. But I continued to lie in bed. I felt stuck, and yet adrift at the same time.

"This," I said to the ceiling in my isolation, "is probably not a good sign."

I am not alone feeling lonely. It's come up in a group chat I am in with friends. The chain is big—full of single and partnered people, and sometimes each can covet another's life even if they wouldn't trade their own. I would say that in the past, the single friends have decidedly come out on top. COVID has shaken the board.

One single friend mentioned she had been going to the drugstore just to be among people for a little while. That afternoon a cashier had made a point of mentioning how many times my friend had been in that week. She said she wasn't sure if she was supposed to take it as judgment, but she was happy the lady recognized her.

"Somebody out there can account for my whereabouts," she joked. "I exist."

It was a line you serve to your friends as an invitation to be told you're definitely not crazy to worry about your presence in the world, and it's silly you worried you were. A lot of the partnered people, mostly with families, hit her back right away with messages along the lines of "That is *deep,* dude." Some threw in a "Don't know what I'd do without my husband" that made me gag.

But I noticed her fellow single friends didn't really chime in at all. I went into reporter mode, hitting some of them individually to ask what they thought and how they were doing.

They immediately hit me back, with variations on the same theme of "too close to home."

I wanted to be a good friend and offer something back other than an empty "I hear you." I had the impulse to hope that I would somehow see my friend Joyce. She would give me the context to help me get it right. But even as I thought, *Joyce will know,* another thought fell down right on top of that one: *Joyce is gone.*

Joyce died in late January, in that pre-COVID time of 2020 that now seems like a naïve blur of ancient days. She died alone at home in bed in West Hollywood after an accidental mixing of substances. She was a nightlife publicist, and since we met in New York in our twenties, she was always at the best parties or throwing them, a gorgeous ball of energy and snark in a little black dress. She was famous here in L.A. as a publicist, and industry news outlets emphasized that she had been "found alone."

"Nobody knew for two days," people repeated to each other. "She lived alone."

To hear a friend spoken of in the past tense so soon already feels like a betrayal of them, but there was a tone to how people spoke of her, tainted with a pity no one felt for Joyce in life. In real time, you could feel people twisting the facts of her vibrant life into a narrative that fit the company town that makes cautionary tales of such women. No man, no kids. Surely, she was hiding some "secret sadness."

The facts of her life were repackaged to craft a final act of comeuppance for the career girl. The Joyce *we* knew came to L.A. to reinvent her life after a messy divorce in her mid-thirties. She wrote her own story, one that didn't involve a specific man, and didn't involve kids, either. It was about chosen family and finding new members to bring into the tribe.

But the media's reinvention of Joyce was that she was heartbroken because she was never able to have a family. Like all good lies, there was a single thread of truth in there. Joyce, a single Filipino woman, was open with her crew that her family often felt that she was doing some sort of dangerous trek into uncharted territory. She told her friends that her parents had fears for her, and the greatest one was that she would die alone. Dying single, however, was *never* her fear.

This hijacking of her narrative in death was so complete that it even began to color our memories of Joyce and what her passing meant to us. Our single friends told me that this tale was their nightmare: "To die alone in yoga clothes, and nobody noticing for days?" The mythmaking around her death also forced the married friends to confront our fears. If the idea of dying alone was, well, a fate worse than death, then we had to examine how a fear of that happening had influenced our choices. In our most honest moments, we might admit that in our thirties we looked around at this musical-chairs game of elimination and worried. We knew there were fewer seats than players, and went to each wedding to watch one more chair taken away. Did we settle, land in a safe, this-will-do spot and tether ourselves to someone for *decades* so we wouldn't be standing alone at the hour of our death? And was it actually worth it?

I found myself staring at Joyce's @goldenladyla Instagram, trying to see if I really had missed some sadness. As I scrolled through the photos, I knew I was probably not alone in doing so. The news reports used her Instagram photos, and one idle click of a photo would bring strangers to her account, a timeline of her life. Maybe at that moment, some other lookie-loo was scrolling alongside me. Someone I'd never meet, who only knew Joyce as a story, might be judging and zeroing in on the same pictures to find fault. Like someone bringing a critical eye to the real estate photos of a house they can't afford.

They saw what I saw: Joyce, with a genuine smile and a pose she'd perfected. Her hand placed on her hip, a slight dip of her shoulder to showcase her long black hair, her angled chin raised to find her light. But what details did strangers fill in for her?

I stopped on a photo of me that Joyce posted at my birthday party just a few months before her death. I am beaming in that picture because Joyce is taking the photo. If something had happened to me, I pictured the lookie-loo trying to decode *my* smile to find secret pain. You can tell whatever story you want about the dead. They are not here to argue. Just as a woman who dies alone in her apartment can't put on the dress she loves, or stage herself to be found. She has to depend upon the kindness and grace of strangers. And count on her friends to seize back ownership of her story to keep it in the family.

Her chosen family.

I called Joyce's best friend, who had been living in Denver. "I was just thinking of her," she said.

"Me, too," I replied. Instead of feeding into the sadness, we reclaimed her pride and her power, sharing stories only sisters know. I asked if she thought Joyce feared dying alone. A long time ago, Joyce made her best friend promise that if anything ever happened to her, she would get to the house before her parents did. "Find anything that might lead my parents to think I was not a good Catholic who remained a virgin for life. Let them hold out hope for their forty-seven-year-old daughter."

"I booked a flight as soon as I found out," her best friend told me. "A deal's a deal."

"That's real," I said.

"It is."

Not was, is. That kind of love is eternal. Joyce didn't fear dying alone any more than she feared living alone. She was single by choice and she loved it, her life no less big and adventurous because she didn't have kids. It served her memory nothing allowing strangers to apply a fear-based method of scoring to decide whether she had won or lost in life.

After that conversation, it was like Joyce had entered the group chat about her life, and her friends worked to reclaim her narrative. We shot down any pity because we carried the real story that Joyce created for herself. Joyce may have died by herself, but she wasn't alone. She was never alone.

I thought about Joyce as I texted my single friends back those few months later. The right thing to say was not "the right thing" to say. It was to listen.

"I'm here if you want to talk," I wrote, adding a funny-face emoji to keep the message from being too weird and earnest.

The phone rang. I picked up.

15

DEAR ISIS

Somebody asked about you again today.

People love you, Isis. When they come up to me in public—
Black people especially—you are who they want to talk about.
Sometimes, who they want to talk *to*. Isis, the cheerleader captain
of the East Compton Clovers in *Bring It On*. A talented girl whose
cheer routines were stolen by the rich white kids at Rancho Carne
High. Whitened up and presented as their own. Do you remember
the words we said, that Friday night in a borrowed high school gym
turned into a film set? "Putting some blond hair on it and calling it
something different." It's the moment everyone calls the confronta-
tion scene, but it's where I made you surrender. When I ad-libbed the
words I thought you needed to say.

The person today, a young Black woman on a Zoom call, thanked me for playing you. "Isis was really a role model for me," she said. "She called people out on their shit and still went on to win."

"She didn't go far enough," I said, so quick the person leaned back from her camera. "She let them off easy."

I had the voice of a mother who expected more from her daughter. I realize that what you did, Isis, confronting Kirsten Dunst's character Torrance about the thievery, is way more than most characters get to do. When it comes to Black characters in TV or film getting to hold white folks accountable, yeah, it was heroic. But it was just a step. It wasn't everything you could have done, and that's because *I* didn't do what I should have done.

If I sound like a disappointed mom, it's because I've always felt I birthed you. It's that way with all the characters I play, though I have never admitted that because it sounds too actor-y. But I feel this most strongly about you, Isis, because I put the words in your mouth. Day in and day out, from the first reading to the set, I crossed out lines and filled in the void they'd left for you. The stuff they gave you to say wouldn't have worked: constant threats of violence in the imagined Ebonics written by people who barely knew Black people. After all, I had to get you to the script's final scene: you at UC Berkeley, an elite school, cheering with Torrance. I knew what it would take for a young Black girl from East Compton to get there.

So that was the goal for you as I rewrote you into existence. To get you where you were going, I made you swallow your anger to be the most palatable version of Black leadership possible. You could point out a wrong and a lack of accountability, but you could not demand it. I had you make all the little compromises and everyday concessions I thought you needed, the ones that I thought I needed to make at one time or another, just so you would be heard.

Here I had the power to make you anything in the world, and I thought I had to make you *worthy*. Of admiration. Of love. So, I made you respectable. And I am so, so sorry.

———

I should start where we met, Isis. We did the reading at a Hollywood theater, an assembly of actors where only a couple of people would end up landing the roles. I wanted this one. Setting aside my need to win everything, which I know we share, I needed the job. This is a big deal, I said to myself, holding the script just before the table read. But those words. Your lines were full of made-up slang that made me cringe.

As the only Black person at the reading, I already felt isolated. I didn't want to read the words on the page, but I knew I had to because this was one step toward securing the offer. In the end, my fear of being maligned by my own community superseded my fear of getting replaced. I couldn't live with facing Black people if I didn't change that dialogue.

So, I said something, and the director, Peyton Reed, said, "Thank you for pointing this out. Let's go line by line and just fix it."

It's part of the *Bring It On* lore, right? Gabrielle Union and Peyton Reed changed the dialogue on shooting days. I've said I wanted to make your character more realistic—more authentically Black—but Isis, one of my chief concerns was getting you to UC Berkeley. Torrance making it there, no one would question. She could use Valley Girl lingo the whole movie and no reviewer would say, "But is she exhibiting enough leadership qualities and intelligence to justify her ending up at an institution like UC Berkeley at the end?" No, she's white. You don't really see Torrance taking AP classes or studying, but *somehow* there's no need to justify whether or not she earned her spot.

You, however, needed to work twice as hard as Torrance to go from East Compton to land in the UC system. You needed to be beyond reproach. Not just as a cheerleader, but as a community leader and student. *And* you had to do all that without sacrificing your Blackness. How was I going to accomplish this for you?

I was twenty-six, and I knew all the extra work I had done myself. I wasn't that far removed from my own journey as a UC student when we shot the film in 1999. That was right after Prop 209 in your home state of California, which banned affirmative action not just in state hiring, but state university admissions. This move greatly reduced the number of Black students in the UC system. UC Berkeley alone showed a 25 percent average drop in Californian Black and Latinx enrollment.

Like so many Black mothers, I was working with the facts at hand. I knew you wouldn't have the advantages of Advanced Placement college prep classes at your school back then. Black and Latinx students in public schools like yours were disproportionately disadvantaged by a lack of access to AP classes. In 1999, the year I created you, the ACLU of Southern California filed a civil rights class action lawsuit, *Daniel v. California,* on behalf of public high school students denied access to AP courses. The ACLU saw the trap you were in: completing an AP course gave students an extra point in the University of California system's calculation of their grade point average, so AP students had the advantage of going over the 4.0 "perfect score." They highlighted a school near yours, Inglewood High, which had three AP courses, while Beverly Hills High offered forty-five. And guess what? The ACLU pointed out that UC Berkeley rejected eight thousand applicants whose GPAs were 4.0 or higher, and instead took the kids with even higher GPAs.

Black girls like you thought they couldn't be less than perfect.

And even that wasn't enough. I had more advantages than you, and I didn't even take AP classes. To give myself even more of an edge—anything to be chosen—I took night classes at a community college my junior and senior years of high school. It was me and Todd Mann, this white kid who had a vintage BMW. Twice a week, we'd drive to Chabot College, a half hour out of town, listening to his tapes of the Jerky Boys and Andrew Dice Clay. We were the youngest students in those classes—history and English—with the oldest being folks in their seventies. They valued the experience, doing the papers just because they wanted to. But you and I *had* to, Isis. Our actions couldn't be driven by interest, but by necessity. Our other classmates could let time slip by, because their lives would be waiting for them, handed to them at graduation. Not us. We had to prove we were worthy.

I decided you had to be studying at night for pre-college credits, too. This would have been off-screen, along with the parents of the Clovers they never showed in the film. I knew you had involved parents. Yes, I created a whole life for you, the girl who the screenwriters didn't bother giving a last name. There was Torrance Shipman, Sparky Polastri, and the Pantones—Cliff and Missy. But us Clovers? Isis, Jenelope, Lafred, and Lava? None.

No surname for you to claim, Isis. Or to claim you. So, you were my daughter alone.

I filled in the lines, putting you in those night classes, actually figuring out how you made it work around cheer practice. I had to instill that discipline in you. After all, I had to prep you not just to get in to UC Berkeley, but to stay. Because I had seen a lot of kids get in—but they couldn't keep up, could they? There's all kinds of reasons why Black and brown kids leave college, not just academic. But you would have to maintain a certain GPA to continue to play sports. And cheerleading, whatever people think of it, is a sport.

Which brings me to the scene everyone memes and loves. The scene so many people congratulate me for. What a proud mother I must be.

We filmed it on a Friday night in a borrowed San Diego high school standing in for East Compton. It was an outdoor shoot, right at the threshold of the gym. This was the scene where I confront Torrance and Missy, played by Eliza Dushku, after they travel to East Compton to watch us cheer. Missy takes Torrance there to show how Big Red, the former captain of the cheerleaders, had actually been ripping off Clover routines for years, the same routines Big Red had passed on to Torrance. They watch us perform and realize their lives are a lie. According to the script, you stop Torrance and Missy as they're slipping out of the gym. You assume they're stealing again, and want whatever videotape they took of the routines you invented.

This was one of the scenes where the Black actresses had to finesse the script day-of to avoid the embarrassing dialogue that was initially written for us. Left to improvise, I had free rein to put words in your mouth and ad-lib your thoughts on cultural appropriation. Not just that: Race and worthiness. Who gets opportunities and why. The scene would give white people a chance to see themselves as complicit in cultural appropriation, but the takeaway for marginalized audiences would be different. It could tell them, "You're not crazy. Your physical and intellectual labor really has been stolen and repackaged for profit. It's real."

I knew it was important, and I felt even more scrutinized because I had friends on set. Dulé Hill and two of my girlfriends, Lacondra and Kristen, had come down to San Diego for the weekend. I knew Dulé from working as two of the few Black people in *She's All That,* a movie for which, by the way, IMDB has no account of our characters' last names, as opposed to the other nine "leads." Lacondra is a super religious girl from the South. She had a boyfriend who was equally religious, but additionally Lacondra was very up front about having a crush on Dulé. Apropos of nothing, she would turn to him to tease in her southern drawl, "Why don't you love me, Dulé?"

I had them stand in Video Village, which is the part of every film set where a large monitor is placed so the crew can watch the movie as it's being filmed. Knowing Dulé was watching added more pressure to get it right. That year he had started filming his role as Charlie on *The West Wing*. It was and is a white show. There were no other Black people on that show but him, so Dulé intimately understood how challenging it was to have conversations like the ones I'd been having on this set. You get a script and there's something in there that doesn't ring true at all or it's problematic. That dance that you have to do, and all the compromises you make.

In the scene, as Jenelope, Natina Reed says to Isis, "Can we just beat these Buffys down so I can go home? I'm on curfew, girl."

Isis, I had you tell Jenelope that hurting them would just clear their consciences about stealing from us. You let Torrance and Missy know the Toros had been stealing from the Clovers for years and profited from things they denied us—championships and ESPN exposure.

We ran through a bunch of takes, and I modulated your anger each time. And each time the director said "Cut," I would go up to Dulé. "What do you think? What do you think?" And "Did I go too far? Is that too much?"

Dulé would just raise his eyebrows like a good therapist. "Is that . . . Do *you* think that's good enough? How do *you* feel?"

I don't know which take it was, Isis, but this is what made it in: "Every time we get some, here y'all come," you say. "Trying to steal it, putting some blond hair on it and calling it something different.

We've had the best squad around for years, but no one's been able to see what we can do. But you better believe all that's gonna change this year. *I'm* captain, and I guarantee you we'll make it to Nationals. So, hand over the tape you made tonight and we'll call it even for now."

We'll call it even. I thought you had to give them grace in the face of the thievery. You had every right to ask them to come forward publicly about what they had done, seek forgiveness, and work toward justice. But I made you educate, yet again, people who absolutely know better and still refuse to do better.

Natina, for one, was not having it. She had her character Jenelope, her child, say, "What? Come on, Isis, let me do this."

I had you refuse. Walk away. "You know what? Let's go."

"Wait a minute," said Jenelope/Natina. "So that's it? We're just gonna let them go?"

"Yeah," I made you say. "Because unlike them, we have class."

I thought surrender was "class." I didn't know that I could give you "class" and dignity while also being very clear about holding people accountable. Beating them up may have been beneath you, but I wish I had even allowed you to be angry. To not muzzle any of that rage, including the justifiable anger of your teammates.

Because that scene at the gym was a rare opportunity for you and them. When you're young and Black and in predominantly Black settings like you had, you don't get to have those confrontations because white folks just aren't around. It's the blues riff taken by the British band and sold back to America, the TikTok girls stealing the Black girl's dance. We don't know it's happening until it's too late. But here *you* had caught them in this moment of potential accountability, and you had to wipe the slate clean.

It was a wrap. As Dulé, Lacondra, and Kristen drove with me

out of the high school parking lot, I was still stuck on it. "I wonder which take they'll use," I said.

And again, "Did I go too far? Did I not go far enough?" Dulé did not answer.

The next afternoon, Dulé and I went to Mission Beach in San Diego with Lacondra and Kristen. As we were walking around the packed beach we came across a Black family reunion. They were a huge family under a banner with their name. They formed a semi-circle around ten family members, who knelt before huge wedges of bright red watermelon.

Dulé said, "Are they—"

"They are," I said.

It was a watermelon-eating contest. They bent forward to devour the watermelon. Dulé and I stood there, watching this real-life version of Black folks from racist jokes and imagery.

"Oh my God," I said. "I can't look." I wanted to put a magic force field around this family gleefully eating that watermelon, cheering each other on. I wanted to save them from all the people on the packed beach watching this dream come true for lovers of stereotypes.

"Why are y'all tripping about watermelon?" asked Lacondra. Kristen, who is biracial, didn't see the harm, either.

"I just can't," I said.

"Eat watermelon?" asked Kristen. "Seriously?"

Lacondra pointed at them, and I resisted the urge to push her arm down. "Their family clearly doesn't have a problem," she said. "So why do you? What do you think it's saying about *you* that you guys are taking this personally? What is wrong with *you*?"

What *was* wrong with me? I was terrified of looking like someone's racist image of the happy Negro eating watermelon. I never ate it, not even cut up on the hottest day. It was one of the many things, all the things, that I robbed myself of enjoying because I was afraid it wasn't *respectable.* But to whom, Isis? I'd placed myself in my own ingenious prison, always seen, always judged. Because *I* was always seeing, and always judging, other Black people.

This family was free. They didn't care about some racist seizing upon this moment as a visual joke, or any Black girl like me being worried about them being seen as caricatures. When really, I was worried about how their actions reflected on *me.*

Isis, I gave you that same fear. I made you as afraid as I was.

———

There was never a real reckoning for you, right? There's the "cheer-off" scene where you and three of the Clovers show up at the Rancho Carne Toros football game during halftime. As the Toros do the cheers they stole, you do them better, but in the stands. The audience does a sort of tennis match spectator back-and-forth between the two teams, but they are scared of us. The takeaway is not, "Wait, these are real stars." It's "Who are these scary Black girls at our white institution?"

Even at Nationals, which you go to only because an Oprah-like benefactor paid your way to be on that level playing field, I made you make space for the white fragility you encountered there. You *won*—your team beat the Toros fair and square, and you had to be gracious about it.

"I respect what you did out there," you tell Torrance. "You guys were good."

"Thanks," says Torrance. "You were better."

I raise your chin, as if this was news that hadn't occurred to you. You answer: "We were, hunh?"

The bashful humility makes Torrance chuckle, and she walks away. Debt paid, conscience clear. They don't have to think about what they did and how it affected the opportunities of a group of Black and brown girls down the freeway.

Now? I would do that line so differently. There would be no surprised "hunh," and certainly no question mark. It would be, "We were." Period. I'd give you the moment to be happy that you were finally being acknowledged as a champion. "Captain to captain," I want you to say to Torrance, "you finally had to do your own work and you came in second. I'm sorry you are faced with the fact that when things are equal, you are not good enough."

I couldn't let you have that. I had to get you to Berkeley, right? We shot the ending with you and Torrance in Berkeley cheer uniforms, playfully squabbling over who would be captain. We filmed at the UCLA campus as a stand-in, and I was proud to be back at my own alma mater. A homecoming for me, and I'd gotten you there. Roll credits.

They cut the scene.

"It really kind of had no place in the movie," the director, Peyton Reed, said in one of the many oral histories of the film. "It really didn't feel like it said anything, or did anything, so we just decided to cut it."

You never made it to Berkeley. Instead they ran a blooper reel, mixed with the cast lip-syncing to the song "Mickey." I get it: it's epic, and it's something people remember.

You know what else people remember? You as a villain.

I once saw a poll of greatest movie villains and there you were. Why? Because you asked for accountability in the most civil tone I could manage? When people do their impersonation of you—*to me!*—it's an aggressive, slang-talking girl threatening violence. I want to ask them, "Uh, show me where I did that? Show me where that was my act." It's interesting how my tone is received and regurgitated. And how you, calmly fighting for credit for your work—fictionally!—were internalized by so much of the audience as scary.

That same unwarranted fear translates into the adultification of Black girls and the criminalization of Black childhood. In New York City elementary and middle schools, Black girls are eleven times more likely to be suspended than their white peers. And a recent Georgetown study of adult attitudes toward Black girls across the nation found a tremendous adultification bias against Black girls as young as *five,* with respondents saying those girls need less nurturing, protection, and support than white girls. A follow-up study sought the comments of older Black girls like you, and they reported harsher treatment and higher standards at school. One of the young respondents said, "I feel like you cannot make mistakes as a Black girl."

I would not let you come anywhere close to a mistake, but the reality is that you can do all the things that white folks tell you that you need to do in order for them to respect you and give you basic-ass human rights . . . and it still won't fucking matter. You're a villain. You are Sandra Bland, calmly asserting her rights to State Trooper Brian Encinia, who pulled her over on a July afternoon in 2015 in Prairie View, Texas. Sandra Bland knew her rights. She *told* him her rights. When Black women assert themselves, that somehow threatens people. This happens in retail situations, corporate offices, and school hallways. A Black woman can be minding her own business, and how she responds to provocation or even a random question will be used against her. When Encinia asked if Ms. Bland was irritated, she calmly said she was. When she wouldn't put out her cigarette, which is not illegal, he decided her tone was combative, and ordered her out of the car. When she refused, he pulled out his Taser and screamed, "I will light you up." In the video, he sounds absolutely unhinged. Minutes later, Encinia hog-tied Ms. Bland on the side of the road. Days later—Isis, she was held for *three days* because of a minor traffic stop—she was found hanging in a jail cell.

It doesn't matter what you say, it matters how you make people feel. And you can't control that. Knowing how you and I would be received, I should have just put the words in your mouth unapologetically.

So, I am here to apologize to *you*. When I said today that you didn't go far enough, that was on me. I failed you and myself. I was the fourth lead, but my face was on the poster. You were the girl with no last name, but the star of every meme. You were only in about a third of the movie, and now I would know to fight for equal time to tell your story. Your iconic moments with the Clovers are what people remember, though I know it's partly that we are bits of Black resistance dropped in the middle of the milk.

Your story, the real one, is that you are amazing *with* your rage. With your disappointment, your heartbreak, and all your complicated feelings. Never in spite of them or because you hid them.

I wish I had just given you the space to be a Black girl who is exceptional without making any kind of compromise. Because that's who I want to be now. That's what *I* am chasing, so much later in life than you: to be exceptional by my *own* standards. Unapologetically me.

I can't make this up to you. You and the movie exist as you were created more than twenty years ago. This apology is a promise to simply do better as I raise two girls now. You would love them. When Kaavia James was on the edge of one year old, someone gave her a baby-sized cheerleader uniform that looked like yours. When she put it on and was into it . . . it was a moment. Because not every outfit gets to live, Isis. Kaav will take something right off if she doesn't like it.

There she was, her little belly sticking out, looking deadpan no matter what new person screamed in delight at the sight of us. She is not the girl who gives the defensive smile, or who worries about the feelings of grown-ups who can take care of themselves. As Black girls, you and Kaav have not been given the space to be unimpressed and unbothered. I need to create it for her. As a teenager, Zaya is her own person and my job is to support her. To do my best to provide the nurturing and support she and countless Black thirteen-year-olds like her do not receive outside the home. But Kaav is reliant on me creating that space while she's a toddler. Since she was born I have made a point of not just dressing her in name-brand clothes or having her hair done perfectly every time I document her. I want her to have the freedom to exist as her authentic self.

You taught me that, Isis. I'll be forever grateful.

I love you.

16

ESCAPE FROM KING'S LANDING

We ran up the hill. The lights of the hotel gleamed above us in the dark. *Get there*, I thought. *It's safe there.* My best friend Larry was behind me, still gripping the beer bottle he had broken to use against the neo-Nazis chasing us. He was the only one of my friends not crying. Thomas, Malika, and Chelsea, just ahead of me, kept looking back to see if those monsters were still behind us.

"Keep going," Larry told us. He didn't need to. We just wanted to make it out of King's Landing alive.

The trip to Dubrovnik had started out so promising. We landed in Croatia that afternoon and went straight from the plane to work. This was June 2019, and I was selling *L.A.'s Finest* to international buyers. My costar Jessica Alba and I had offered to attend an industry convention in Dubrovnik as a pit stop during our European press tour. We had a strong pilot to show off, a drama about two cops in the *Bad Boys* universe of Jerry Bruckheimer. Jessica and I killed it, and by the end of the day, we were so successful we gave each other a high-five, like the end of the montage when the plucky entrepreneurs sit back and count their money.

We each had our little teams—a glam squad and publicist in tow—and each had different plans for our one night in Dubrovnik. Jess and her group wanted to do more of a high-end tour of the city. If she was doing the Goop version, I joked to my team, "we're doing the Poop version." My team's friendship runs years deep. There was my best friend and hairdresser, Larry, my makeup artist Malika, my stylist Thomas, and my publicist, Chelsea. Whenever we travel together we are all about a good time. And that meant going to King's Landing.

We were all superfans of *Game of Thrones,* which shot the show's King's Landing castle and village scenes in Dubrovnik's Old City. Our hotel looked out on the giant medieval fortress, a maze of cobblestone side streets and red-roofed buildings surrounded by a mile-long wall. Picture Medieval Times meets Disneyland, right on the edge of the Adriatic Sea.

All five of us gazed down at King's Landing during our dinner at the hotel restaurant. We were out on the terrace, and the air had cooled to the high seventies, the waters of the Adriatic darkening to a deep blue as the sunset made the sky orange and purple.

"This *place,*" I said. I was still done up from the conference, serving glam*our* but now dressed down in pants and sneakers. I kept shaking my head back, loving the sideswept chop of a bob that Larry had given me just a few days before.

"It's gorgeous," said Larry, seated next to me. He moved in his chair, wearing a mesh shirt only he could pull off, absently picking up the rhythm of the music around us. I have known Larry since my *Bring It On* days, when I met him as a dancer performing at a car show with my costars, the singing group Blaque. Even after he transitioned to hair, it's still been a habit of his to adjust to the beat around him and make it his own.

Sitting across from us was Thomas, serving Cape Cod twink, and Malika, still dressed in her go-to work look of black shorts and a black sleeveless top. The fifth member of our little band was Chelsea, my publicist, who'd been with us for years but still seemed like the kid sister. Her hair was long and hanging down her face with a slight curl, a newer Bohemian version of Edie Brickell, or maybe a biracial cousin of Haim.

We were on our second bottle of wine and the chef realized we were an up-for-anything crew. He kept bringing us things that weren't on the menu, pairing the dishes with wines from the cellar. Still, our eyes kept returning to the lights of King's Landing below us.

"I want to be there," I said in a Disney princess voice, speaking for all of us. "Take me down *there*." We asked our new friend the chef how far of a walk it would be, and he said five minutes.

"We could get a nightcap there," said Thomas.

"What if there's fans?" Chelsea asked me.

"Oh," I said, joking. "*Well.* It's a risk we'll have to take for King's Landing."

"We're going," said Larry.

In no time we were settled up, photos taken with the staff, and halfway down the hill, just us. Even before we got into the Old City, everywhere we looked was an Instagram moment: "That's a picture . . . that's a picture." We were already a group primed for impromptu photo shoots, so this was like a social media theme park. Still, we were quiet, because we were aware that as much as this was a place for tourists, more than one thousand people still called the Old City home. You might even say we were reverent in this place, because we were so devoted to this show. Our last view of these streets we walked upon had been seeing them incinerated under the fire of Daenerys and her dragon.

We were just inside the huge door letting you in to King's Landing when a tour bus pulled up to belch out a long line of white teens. They were probably high school seniors or university freshmen, coming right toward us. We paid them no mind, going on about our Lannisters at Leisure photo shoot. Then I heard a voice from the group.

"Oh my God, there's so many of them." I couldn't place the accent, whether it was English or Australian, but it was in the international language of disdain. We turned to look behind us, to see whatever it was they were talking about. Sparrows? White Walkers? Wildlings?

They were talking about us.

As they barreled their way in to King's Landing, one guy was pushed out of line to be closer to us. He recoiled, and curled his lip into a sneer.

"*What,* is Obama in town?"

The teens began laughing, each trying to be louder than the other until it was a forced jeering directed at us. My team and I froze, more out of confusion than fear. They started filing into a club right inside the gate. The Arya Stark in us rose, and we did a delayed stutter-step move of "Oh, no the fuck you won't," toward them. Horrible music bled from the club, a relentless *doochie-doochie-doochie* beat.

"We're going in there," I said. "Fuck that." Malika rolled her eyes, and I sighed. "You're right. Go in and pay our money? To do what?"

"Let's go see the rest of King's Landing," said Chelsea.

We were just a little bit into King's Landing when we ran into Jessica and her team leaving dinner.

"Oh my God," she said. "That place was wonderful. Best time. Best service." They were heading to bed at the hotel. In Jessica's group, she had an Asian makeup artist, a Mexican hairstylist, and two white people. They were an undeniably ethnic bunch, and this felt like a vote for our crew. If *they* had a good time in King's Landing . . .

Those were just some kids, we decided. "Outside agitators," I joked.

Now we just had to find a good local place for our nightcap. We kept looking, but nothing said King's Landing—every place we passed was just the generic Euro tourist bar. And we nixed any place playing that *doochie-doochie* dirge of electronic music. Which did not leave much—it seemed King's Landing was one big house party.

I asked Larry to stand by a beautiful arch in a wall covered in the patina left by centuries of rain. I wanted to get a picture of him looking so regal in a fairy tale setting. I squatted to get the angle just right. Out of the corner of my eye I saw Thomas move to stand between me and two men who'd stopped to look at us. I turned to watch us being watched.

Thomas did something, some subtle bit of body language that caused them to shrug and move on. He turned back to us, and for a second his face still had the hardness he'd shown these men. Thomas Christos Kikis's parents are Greek immigrants who came to Tampa and got into the restaurant business. Growing up he spent a lot of time in Greece, a neighbor of Croatia. Whatever had transpired between them was in an unspoken cultural language that Thomas still had use of.

"What happened there?" I asked Thomas.

"Nothing," he said, but looked back to watch them continue to walk. We did, too, entering a large square, one of the two we'd seen from above in the hotel. I thought about how the five of us had all had to live in two worlds at some point. To translate our lives for safety. Thomas grew up gay in America and in Greece. There was me going from Black Omaha to white Pleasanton. Larry living under the constant threat of violence growing up gay and Black on the west side of Chicago, then working in extremely wealthy spaces in L.A. Chelsea was biracial but spent most of her life in white spaces. And Malika, who was raised in Ohio but did the reverse Great Migration of going to college in Alabama, where she was reminded of the Confederacy at every turn.

And here we were in this ancient city, yet another world for us. The only thing missing was the dragons.

"Wait," said Malika. "Is that—"

We gasped. The stairs. *The* stairs where Cersei Lannister, the ultimate brotherfucker, begins her walk of shame through the alleyways of King's Landing to the Red Keep. We took turns as Cersei, grabbing tissue to ball up and hurl as rocks to play the villagers taunting her with "Shame! Shame!"

We followed Cersei's footsteps right into getting lost in the quiet medieval village. It was getting late, and we still hadn't found a place for a final drink of the night. Around us was a maze of elevated alleyways. I looked up one corridor to see what appeared to be rainbow lights around the door of a bar. When I was a little girl, my mother always told me that if I was ever lost in a big city, "Look for the rainbow flag." She believed in the goodness of the LGBTQ+ community, and knew there would be protection and direction there. I have always found this to be true.

"Did we just find the gay bar at King's Landing?" I asked.

"Probably *the* gay bar of Dubrovnik," muttered Thomas. We walked up the narrow alleyway, toward the rainbow lights like we'd found Oz. The cobblestone corridor was lined with doors and alcoves, and we finally started to see the locals. People popped their heads out to scowl at us, almost like this was part of the *Game of Thrones* experience, latecomers to the mob growling at Cersei. They really did seem angry. Again, we were dead quiet, so it was simply the sight of us that brought this reaction. Still, we thought maybe this was part of the thrill. We were on a ride.

There were tall tables outside the bar, and more people looking up from their drinks to stare at us. The alleyway felt more closed in now. We could hear that signature house music from inside. I shrugged. "Let's see what they got," I said.

We stepped into darkness. I wondered how anyone could even order or find a seat. As our eyes began to adjust, the place didn't look like any gay bar we'd ever seen. We craned our heads, peered in the dark to find an open area, and saw that a good portion of the crowd had turned to stare at us.

"I'm going to the bar," said Larry, paying the people no mind—not even hinting that he'd seen them. "Beers?"

From where we stood at the entrance, I watched him at the bar, slightly bebopping to the house music, trying to catch the vibe of the place. The bartender ignored him at first, then she finally ambled over, looking like the angry bus driver on *South Park*. As he ordered, the man next to him heard his voice and turned to look. Larry didn't see the man move inches over, almost crowding the guy next to him so as not to be near Larry. Like dominoes, the people seated at the bar looked at Larry with daggers in their eyes.

"I've gotta go to the bathroom," Malika said, slipping out from behind me.

"We'll stay here until you and Larry get back," I said. "If we see a place to sit we'll get you."

That left Chelsea, Thomas, and me. I was thinking of the scene in *48 Hrs.* where Eddie Murphy takes Nick Nolte to the redneck bar to show him racism. "This is not a gay bar, is it?" I said. Thomas shook his head. He understood this crowd better than me, and his face was taking on that steeliness I'd seen when the two men were staring at us.

I saw some people get up to leave their table, so I stepped forward to grab it. But when they turned and saw us, they changed their mind and sat down again, facing us like there was going to be a show.

I was about to go over to Larry, tell him we should just go, when Malika came flying at us.

"What's wrong?" I asked. She looked so stricken I thought she'd been hurt.

"Come here and look at this," she said, grabbing my hand to drag us into the hallway leading to the kitchen and bathrooms.

"*Malika*. What *happened*?" I said.

"Wait," she said, grabbing her phone to turn on its flashlight. "*This.*"

She shone the light on the walls, and it was the jump scare of horror movies. The walls were covered in Jim Crow memorabilia.

White-eyed Black mammies and jockeys stared back at us, a picture of a Black baby sucking a bottle that said "INK." A drawing of a little Black child devouring fruit under the words DIXIE BOY. Everywhere you looked a new degradation, all of it Americana.

"They had to import their racism," I said.

"Jesus," Malika said, taking pictures. She lowered her phone, and the light briefly fell on a woman entering the hallway. We jumped, and the woman practically hissed.

"We have to go," I said. "We have to fucking *go*."

Malika pointed to the bathroom door. "Somebody was real mad I was in there," she said. "I know they called me a nigger."

"Was it like 'blah blah blah nigger' or did they say 'nigger' in Croatian?" I asked, but did not wait for the answer. In any language, you know when you're called a nigger. We went to go back to our spot by the door so Larry would find us, but there were more people now, taking up that space. They had the same scowl, looking us up and down as we hugged the wall near the door.

Here came Larry, expertly carrying five bottles. "Here's your beers," he said, his voice clipped. "Let's drink and let's just go."

Malika was already holding up her phone to show him the pictures. "Larry, look at this shit," I said. His eyes narrowed, and he pulled his head back. "Here?" he asked.

As our own eyes adjusted, we realized it wasn't just the hallway. The whole place was covered in racist decorations, like trophies of past kills. And we could see our fellow patrons seeing us seeing that. As we pointed, they popped wry grins, like, "Yup. And?"

"Stay behind me," Larry said to us, quietly, trying to sound casual as he directed us outside the bar to one of the picnic tables. The alleyway now seemed even more narrow, and there were people standing around.

"We should go," said Chelsea.

"They're not gonna run us out of here," said Larry, placing our drinks on the table. His voice was measured but direct. This was the Larry of the west side of Chicago, who ended fights he didn't ask for, and who had watched the older sister he idolized, who was trans, have to do the same every day of her life. "We're not gonna run. Let's gather ourselves. We're gonna finish our drinks, and then we're gonna leave."

I was scared. "Go ahead," Larry said, looking right at me. "Finish your drink." But he wasn't drinking. He held his bottle tight by the neck, ready to draw as he turned to watch the people watching us. There was a group of large men with shaved heads, leering at us. They had a tone of playful murder in their eyes, making a game of trying to scare us. When that didn't get the effect they wanted, they upped the ante. Two of the men made a slow show of lifting their sleeves to display tattoos of swastikas.

"Jesus," I said.

At that, two of them started to get up.

"Okay," Larry said, still casual. "On second thought, fuck that."

Glass shattered. In one fell swoop, Larry broke the bottle against the wall. Now they were all up.

"Walk down the hill," Larry quietly commanded us, staring straight ahead. "Don't look at anybody, don't say shit."

We did as we were told. As he held these men at bay with the bottle, he walked backward. "Don't run," he said. "Just keep walking." Thomas, Chelsea, and Malika were in front of me, and kept turning back to look. They were crying. Seeing that, my own terror mixed with a confused rage. Was it just fun for these people to menace us? Or was it not enough that they had intimidated us into leaving? Maybe they really did want to hurt us.

Going down the alley to the square, I saw why Larry didn't want us to run. The corridor was a gauntlet of people in alcoves. Anyone of them could stop us, grab at us, and then what? What would these men do to us? I pressed my elbows to my sides.

I could see the square. I felt like we had a chance if we made it out of the alley to the square. As we got closer, I saw a cop in the distance. He wasn't looking our way. His arms were crossed. We were getting closer. He would have to do something, right? He could—

He turned. Sneered, and glanced at the men behind us.

Then he looked away.

King's Landing was now a ghost town. The skinheads were shouting at us. I could see the lights of our hotel in the distance above us. I pointed, barely able to talk, and we moved in that direction. My mind went to Kaavia James, who had just started to crawl. I'd been afraid she'd become an expert while I was gone. I wanted to see that.

We fled through the gate of King's Landing and started up the hill to the hotel. I was in a full sweat. We were out of breath, but the skinheads had stopped because they got what they wanted: us gone.

We didn't utter a word to each other, all of us numb and in shock.

For most of my life, I have gamed out worst-case scenarios with if-this, then-this precision. Like, "If I end up in a bar that I thought was a gay bar, but it's full of Nazis who have decorated the place in Jim Crow memorabilia . . . then I know what I'd do: I'd kick everybody's ass."

The truth is harder. *No, you're outnumbered. And you're not trying to die in a fucking Croatian bar in King's fucking Landing.*

We entered the hotel and said nothing to the front desk. Just slinked in, our tails between our legs. I caught us in a mirror, and we looked like we'd lost a fight, even though they didn't get a punch in.

I didn't want to be alone and neither did the others. We all hung out in my room, too wired to sleep. Larry remained rigid, his adrenaline ebbing slowly. I curled my body into a chair, making myself as small as possible.

I got out my phone to research Croatia, and spent the night going down a rabbit hole learning about the country and its immigration policies. Because when you are confronted with that kind of perceived threat of violence, it plays with your head. You wonder what you might have done to incite it, when really, you just existed in a public space that did not want you. In 2019, there'd been a spike in nationalistic hate crimes in Croatia, one of the whitest countries in the world with Croats making up more than 90 percent of the population, and Serbs being its largest "minority." That night I read countless accounts of Black travelers horrified by racism in Croatia, including apparent poisoning of meals at restaurants where waiters stood around and giggled as Black people ate. Beatings, intimidation, and refusal of service.

I recited them to the group. "Black, brown, and gay people," I said, "need travel services that tell you, 'These people don't want you there. Fuck what the tourism bureau tells you—*this* is what will happen.'"

The next morning, we were off to London, but we'd lost something. Not our innocence—none of us are naïve—but our wanderlust. That feeling of wanting to escape into a place and immerse yourself in its culture. Growing up Black and/or queer in America, you always think it must be better for you somewhere else. You see pictures of Nina Simone and James Baldwin smiling in the sunshine being so loved in the south of France, Paul Robeson playing to sell-out audiences in Spain . . . and you say what I said when I saw King's Landing: "Take me there. Take me fucking *there*."

We think it has to be better somewhere else, but it's only when we leave that we really understand how anti-Blackness and bigotry are so ingrained in the white supremacy that fuels colonialism. The five of us got this early in our upbringing, living our lives in two worlds.

Now we'd crossed an ocean and a sea, and were met with the mammy and Jim Crow caricatures we thought we'd left. Home-grown racism sold back to us like McDonald's.

We left Croatia, probably never to return, which is what they wanted. After London we were on to Monaco, then Cannes. These spaces were white, but my fame and money trumped all. For now, my team and I had the right currency. But in a flash, again, that could suddenly not matter. We knew that now. I had fame and money on that night in Dubrovnik, and it didn't matter. All that mattered was that my friend in his mesh top was willing to fight our way out. We knew when to run.

Dwyane brought Zaya and Kaavia James to meet me in the south of France, where James Baldwin and Nina Simone had been neighbors. A commercial Dwyane had done was up for awards at the Cannes Lions festival, and we were treated like Black royalty. Waiters cooed over Kaav at breakfast, smiled at Zaya, and asked for selfies with Dwyane.

But I found myself holding Kaavia James everywhere we went. I wanted the weight of her, the entirety of her, safe in my right arm. I kept my other arm free. To do what? To grab a bottle to break? What was I getting ready for? And what, as a Black woman in America, and now the world, did I always have to be in a state of readiness for?

When Kaav strained at my arm, reaching down at the floor, I knew she wanted to practice her crawling. To see the world on her terms. But I wanted her up high with me, where she was safe.

"You just want to explore, don't you?" Zaya said to Kaav.

I reluctantly put her down. "I get it," I said.

17

HOW TO PITCH YOUR LIFE

At first, it's simply flattering when people ask you for career advice. You tuck a lock of hair behind your ear, and say, "Well." And then you look at this person, young or old, and you feel the weight of their hope. Yes, there may be questions about dealing with a toxic workplace or troubleshooting issues with a coworker, but often they are talking about a dream. They want to be seen and heard, in whatever their endeavor.

I have seen this up close the last couple years with my production company. I bring a "to whom much is given, much is required" sense to the work of helping writers and artists develop and sell their projects. I now get to do what people did for me; the people who came before me and didn't just watch me struggle but offered advice. As a boss, I want to provide more opportunities for women of color, and for LGBTQ+ communities—really any marginalized voice. I find the projects and people others overlook, so new stories can be told.

That means I get to be in the room when that magic moment happens and a pitch takes off. A pitch is just a presentation of an idea. It can be anything, but in my case, I am watching people pitch film and TV projects, whole worlds they have created. They can share these stories with a larger audience if they can just get the gatekeepers in the room to believe in them.

Recently I watched a woman I mentored land the deal in the room. This was her fourth time pitching, and the other three times it just hadn't been a good fit or she got in her own way. In one, her voice shook, and then it shook her and she couldn't get past it. In another, a guy was on his phone most of the time. But I believed in her and her pilot. She'd been hot in town briefly when she was young, a time when people can prize your sexy over your talent. She told me that when the sexy faded, she had the same talent, but not as much interest. I joked to her that I had a lot of experience going from it girl to shit girl.

"You only need one yes," I had reminded her a few times. And we could feel it coming right there, in that fourth pitch. What was on the page, that magic, was now in the room. My producing partner and I exchanged a smile. We had been her own personal cheering section in these rooms, but now she was flying on her own.

She has been on my mind because I knew she was close to giving up. She just needed someone like me to believe in her. I am not someone who drinks from the Think Positive mug, but I have found success helping people find *their* success by giving positive, constructive criticism. It doesn't have to be a death blow or some insulting shit somebody's never gonna get over. Over time, I have figured out what different people need in order to get over the hump, and to be acknowledged. To be *released*. Whatever you're pitching—your story, your investment opportunity, your business, your life—I want you to win. Here's what I know:

1. FIND YOUR REAL PEOPLE

Have you ever noticed how mediocre people keep getting breaks? It's because there's a buddy system to every industry, not just mine, so known quantities continue to get deals even as they rack up failures. Mediocre people look after their own, promoting each other and giving each other work. They don't want to look farther than the end of their nose to find talent, and they firmly believe that their friends happen to be the best qualified for the job. A show about the Ozarks? They know a guy they came up with in L.A. who'd have fun with "that world." A show about Dominicans in Spanish Harlem? Their all-white friends are just the thing. They don't really want to do a search because they might find out they're not the most qualified person for the job they have, either.

What if you stop trying to appeal to that closed-off crew, and instead focus on the people who you want to hang with? The people I find or who are drawn to me are mostly either literally brand new to the industry and have never been staffed on a show, or they are marginalized people who have never had someone backing them up. But we find each other because we are like-minded people who are really about the liberation of marginalized folks. We are on the same fucking page, even if we have never met before. We are bound by our passion, which is stronger and more nourishing than a "brand."

This isn't just about Hollywood and writers' rooms. When I talk about finding your people, I mean look around you. They're the people from school or your job in any industry and at any stage of your life—the ones you create with or you run ideas by because you value their feedback. They're not in the spotlight yet, either, but that doesn't matter if you're looking for the people who are not lit from above, but lit from within. The Avengers you assemble don't have to be golden by the standards of the industry you are breaking in to. They just need to have the same work ethic as you, and believe in effective communication and positive affirmation.

And here's the key: don't trade them in once you make it. There's this notion that as you ascend or expand, these people either fall away beneath you or they become your competitors. No, keep these people with you, so you all can draw upon each other for encouragement and support.

2. EXPAND YOUR DREAM TO INCLUDE OTHERS

For a long time, I carried a quote around with me. "I wrote my first novel because I wanted to read it." It's Toni Morrison, of course, talking about publishing *The Bluest Eye* at age thirty-nine. Little Black girls did not exist in many books then, except as window dressing or props. Certainly no one had tried to capture the vast landscapes of their interior lives. And so, *she* did.

As you pursue this impulse to create what you need to see, even if it's just your own achievement, I guarantee you that you will be stronger in doing so if it's to share it with your community and chosen family. I recently relaunched my hair-care line Flawless. The initial 2017 launch had done well financially, but the line didn't really reflect my values. I realized that if I was creating a product for my hair, my first order of business in reclaiming my company was to become Black-owned, Black-led, and Black-marketed. I also wanted to serve my community by not increasing my profit margin through price gouging.

Yes, there's added pressure when you're representing something larger than yourself, but so often that gets put on you anyway. People will ask you, "How does it feel to represent . . ." You have an opportunity to claim your people at the beginning of your journey, and draw strength from them as you do right by them.

3. BE YOUR OWN "YES"

The goal of pitching a TV or film project is to get more than one "yes." Ideally, you want to be able to pick your perfect partner in getting your ideas aired, and also, it's always fun to have a bidding war. But the most important component I've seen is what that first "yes" does for the person pitching. They do their best work in the room because they have been released from the need to be chosen. At that point, they are just pitching out of passion.

So, give a yes to your motherfucking self before you're even in the room. When your success is you, that is not contingent on needing to hear "yes, we're buying it" from anybody. You make that "yes" less important, and free yourself of needing it so badly. Yeah, it's nice, but it's not necessary to keep your passion and dream alive.

Believing in yourself sounds gauzy and spiritual, but it has practical applications. It affects voice quality. You remove the tremor that comes from nerves, and you eliminate the filler language and those long pauses you use when trying to gather your thoughts. You don't get thrown by the faces looking back at you, or the follow-up questions they throw at you. You own your story already, and lots of confidence comes from that.

All because you chose your damn self.

4. QUESTIONS ARE INVITATIONS, NOT CHALLENGES

When we're in that period and mindset after the first "yes," I see people react differently to questions from gatekeepers. They are no longer questions on a quiz or some form of attack, but thoughts to be considered from a potential investor. From someone so interested in the idea you have created that they want to know more.

The same goes for any feedback. You can be strengthened by hearing what is not working or landing in the way you want. Examine it and decide what you're gonna take and what you're gonna discard. When I see someone acknowledge someone's concern about a project rather than fold or become defensive, it's like I'm watching a giant being made.

And yes, in any position or industry, there is going to be rejection. They threw a lemon at you, and now you have an opportunity to hand it back to them and, say, "Make me some lemonade." The lemonade of feedback is the fresh insight into why you didn't close the deal to get the job this time. Turn them into a focus group so you can anticipate these issues in other situations.

5. LEAVE YOUR HEART IN THE ROOM

I've wanted every job that I went out for. I laugh when people ask if I remember any roles I didn't get. If I got dressed and went somewhere, it meant I wanted the role, so of course I remember them. As an actress, it's hard for a grown Black woman to find roles that are nuanced and complex.

If you want something, give yourself permission to go all out for the opportunity and leave your heart in the room. I love watching people add music to a pitch, and visuals as a seasoning to the mix. They can stand up and be animated because they respect themselves; they're presenting passion, not clownery. Let's say you're in one place and you want to get to the next level. Stand up and be animated. Don't worry about how you look or how you are being received. Focus only on your intention, which is to put your whole, full, passionate self into the pitch. How it's received is none of your business. Granted, if the feedback is, "You walked in there and you were a damn clown," rethink it. I don't want to send you down the wrong path. But you might be great, if you dare.

I hear my shy friends getting nervous out there. If you're someone who is scared of public speaking or speaking one-on-one with a boss or someone hiring you, you need to acknowledge that to yourself and, if you need to, to them. Do not be afraid to use notecards. Here's the secret: if you want to be seen in a leadership role, the thing about good leaders is they acknowledge their weaknesses. Those notecards are an acknowledgment that (a) it's something that I'm working on and (b) I am staying on track so I can keep this *meeting* on track and I don't waste your time. They are no reflection of a lack of preparedness or passion.

6. BE ON TIME

That's it. Whatever you're trying to do, just be on time. It's such a rarity in the world that people will trust you more. It'll be you and the sun—the only things people count on to show up. So, shine.

18

THE VOICE OF WISDOM

People make fun of trigger warnings, I know. There are a lot of ass-holes out there.

For me, content warnings give me the opportunity to assess my state of being and whether I want to engage with the author or speaker in that moment. It's the respect of consent. I want to provide one here: in this chapter I will be discussing thoughts of suicide. Passive suicidal ideation, to give you the term that was given to me.

———

Some years back, I began having irregular periods. Which, if you have gotten this far in the book, you know means that I was *having* my period. They were so painful that I was diagnosed with perimenopause. I had never heard that term, though I knew what menopause was. Or at least I thought I did. Looking back, I realize I had only a vague notion, one that was based on bits of asides overheard from my mother when she was in her fifties, or jokes on TV about *older* women. Not sexy young bitches who post thirst traps and want people to see their ass.

So, I learned perimenopause is the time before menopause, characterized by irregular periods. Not much else. For some women, this phase is very short, and for some it can stretch over years. I had never had regular periods, so I didn't investigate it any further since I didn't really notice symptoms. You can also have hot flashes, hair loss, mood swings—basically the classic symptoms used to describe menopause, except for one critical thing: the way you know you're going from perimenopause to menopause is when you don't have your period for twelve months. If you go a full year without your period, it's on.

This fall, I was at the eleven-and-a-half-month mark without my period.

Well, I guess I will be in menopause in my forties, I said to myself.

And then, out of the motherfucking blue, my period showed up. "Hey girl! It's been so long, let's catch up. Cancel your plans, because we need to make up for lost time."

Oh, she was back. This was painful, with heavy bleeding, and along with it came additional hair loss. The crazy hormonal fluctuation made me bloated to a point that I looked like I was either back for another round of IVF or well into my second trimester.

In the midst of this joy, I had a massive blowout with Dwyane. He has a friend who I do not care for, and he had invited this man over to our house knowing I didn't want his energy in my home. I didn't even know until the motherfucker arrived. I felt blindsided, but Dwyane has a filing cabinet of things labeled: "The Absence of Truth Is Not a Lie." Basically, he feels an omission of information is not a lie, and if I am curious about something, say, a guest list, I have a responsibility to ask. He shrugged, storing it with omissions he found harmless, and I seethed. The situation was something he found so small, but to my mind, it represented a fundamental problem in our marriage.

I punished him with silence, which is extreme for me. I was conscious enough to know that my reaction didn't actually match what happened. But once I stopped talking to him, it made sense. I had a vague feeling that I needed to cut him out. That if he was ever going to understand how angry I was, I needed to make him feel bad.

Two days into silence, maybe three, I was at the sink when it came to me.

If you were dead, he would feel really bad. It was a phrase in my mind, clear, calm, and direct.

I physically shook my head, turned the water off and then on again.

You should probably die. Then your point would be made. The voice was final. It had gone through the options, run the numbers. This was the answer.

I recognized that voice. It wasn't scary or the least bit foreign to me, because it was the voice that has walked me through my entire life. We all have it. When you're young, it's the voice of pure instinct. You're walking down the street and pass a house that has bad juju. The voice says, *Watch yourself.* It's the voice inside you that knows the deal before you do.

When I haven't listened to that voice, bad things have happened. I've pretended not to hear it tell me someone was lying to me, to cut my losses when I kept investing in something broken. That voice said, *Run out the back,* when my rapist walked in the store when I was nineteen. I walked to the front.

By the time a woman gets to her upper forties, she has learned to trust that voice, or she regrets it. It's no longer just instinct, but wisdom. *You know exactly how this is gonna go,* it says. Or, *Passive aggressive is the way to go with this one.* Sometimes, the voice takes stock of a situation you can't imagine coming back from, and it gives you the final answer. *You've survived worse.* And *Go on, bitch. Show them.*

And now this voice that had proven itself worthy of all my trust was telling me to die.

"I don't want to," I almost said aloud. Not in a scared or dramatic way. More confused that this was now an option on the table when I'd never been suicidal before. And now it was not an option, it was *the* option. My inner voice responded to this confusion as it always does, with a clear plan that cut through any wishful thinking.

You should die.

———

I continued with the day, distracting myself. I was still bleeding heavily from my period. I breezed by Dwyane like a ghost with a shake of my head, thinking, *If I was dead, he would feel really terrible.*

Somewhere in the part of my mind that wasn't under this dark fog another, quieter voice spoke up. "That's not right, girl," it said. "You don't really wanna die, bitch."

The voice, calm: *Yeah, but it's not about what you want.*

I busied myself, but kept returning to the feeling that I'd gotten bad news. News that mattered to me, but to no one else. Nothing to share. Kaavia James fussed about something, and I handed her my phone to quiet her. I was conscious enough to wait for that inner voice to run its usual cost-benefit analysis about my parenting decisions. The voice would usually say, *Look, do what you need to do.* Or more pointedly, *You just played yourself. Now she'll always expect the phone.*

Silence.

Later, I turned down the light in Kaavia James's room for her nap. Standing at her doorframe, I looked back at her.

They'd all be better off, the voice said. *If you disappear, everyone's life gets better.*

The smaller part of my brain again piped in. "That's not how that works," it said. "Wait, hold on." I picked up my phone. I called my therapist.

I need to say here that I have had a lifetime of therapy. I am privileged with that experience, and I believe it helped me override the system.

"Something's not right," I said. I explained these thoughts. "This isn't me. But it *is*. It's real, and it keeps coming. I'm sure it has something to do with my period returning after eleven and a half months. It's crazy painful."

My therapist told me it was likely perimenopausal depression, and as we talked more, it was clear I was having passive suicidal ideation. The word "passive" implies that this is more a hopeless wish than an "active" one where there are plans and methods considered. We started with increased talk therapy and treating some of my other symptoms holistically, which I will get to. But first I went down the rabbit hole researching perimenopause and depression.

One of the first things I learned was that perimenopausal depression *exists*. I had never heard of it. But I certainly had the related symptoms of depression, anxiety, insomnia, and difficulty concentrating. According to a ten-year study published by the CDC in 2020, the suicide rate among females is highest for those aged forty-five to sixty-four. (If anyone asks you, male suicide is highest for those aged seventy-five and over.) I thought about women in the public eye who had died by suicide—like fashion designers Kate Spade, fifty-five, and L'Wren Scott, forty-nine. In the aftermath, each had people, both journalists and friends, piece together their lives to figure out how their circumstances drove their actions. People centered on the men in their lives, and I realized how often women's depression is ascribed to the actions of men and families around them. This is the time long-term marriages break up, kids leave nests. We focus on the external features of women's lives, and ignore the interior. There's this huge surge and retreat of hormones, not seen most likely since puberty and pregnancy and childbirth, but no one pays any attention to how that affects your brain chemistry and mental health. Like all of women's work, it's invisible.

That's because while perimenopause and menopause happen in women's bodies, science has focused on treating the symptoms that matter most to men and whether or not they want to fuck us. Low libido, fertility, vaginal dryness, signs of aging, hair loss . . . We even focus on hot flashes because it's a spectacle that others have to witness. People are *embarrassed* for you, and you have to dig deep into medical studies to find hot flashes' relation to cardiovascular health risks and energy depletion. You can't expect much, since modern science still doesn't fully know what role hormonal changes play in hot flashes. Even the Mayo fucking Clinic has to rely on a hunch. Instead, we only need fixes for those symptoms a man will notice and care about. "How's your pussy feeling? No, not to *you,* silly. To a penis."

We put money and research into what we value. Half of the human race has been hitting menopause since we've lived long enough to get there. And what do we have to show for it? Even the existing literature about "the Change" is full of rah-rah books that amount to handing you a mug with the label, "It's not a hot flash! It's a power surge." They focus on hiding symptoms and still being sexy. Remaining an option for a man. And it's confusing because this is a time that we are often cast aside and made to feel invisible. "I'm glad you no longer have vaginal dryness, ma'am, but I'm gonna trade you in for the eighteen-year-old anyway. Her face doesn't have any stress lines." Misogyny is already enough of a fucking stressor.

And because no one is talking about the internal changes, you start to feel like what is happening is just in your head, and you *are* going crazy. Feelings of isolation and paranoia take hold. You rack your brain trying to think of the thing you did to deserve this, because this has to be a consequence of some sort of action. But your action is just living. Aging.

As long as we don't talk about any of this, it is so easy for that isolation to cause you to fuck around or kill or harm yourself. We talk about the repercussions of women committing suicide in their forties. They are seen as selfish for leaving their kids behind, caring more about their pain than their responsibilities to family. Their actions are attributed to a character issue, rather than a hormonal imbalance that is causing internal struggles. Challenges that could be addressed if we demanded the language and research to tackle them. I want to stand up for those women, too. Because my instinct was telling me to disappear. It told me, clear as day, in a voice that had so many times steered me right: *If you care as much as you say you do, you'll make their lives easier by killing yourself.*

The voice was still there as I did my googling. But the voice no longer knew everything, because *I* knew something. I did not want to kill myself. The churn of hormones in my body was temporarily making me feel hopeless. There was help, and things I could do, and most of all it was not just in my head.

I don't want to give the impression I think strength is what saved me. I've had lifelong access to therapy, and it was a life preserver I could hold on to. When I learned my issue was from perimenopause and that I shared the issue with countless people I've never met, I knew that it would be wrong not to at least try to push the life preserver your way. And if I'm pushing, I might as well swim it over to you. And now that we're sharing this thing, we could look at each other and say, "We're going to get each other through this." And, "Ain't this some shit?"

―――

When I began talking about perimenopause, I started with my friends. The people in my grown-women group chat range in age from forty to forty-nine. We were all experiencing some symptom, mild or major, of perimenopause, but we weren't having focused discussions around it. I was terrified that someone else might be feeling what I was. I also knew I needed their support.

What stuns me still is that we are smart women, yet we knew so little. This reminded me of bringing my big sister's Judy Blume book to the monkey bars to share with girls at school in order to figure out the mysteries of what happens between penises and vaginas. Or how I was completely clueless about my period and lacked basic knowledge about how to better navigate that transition. This past year we learned about the existence of UFOs, but motherfuckers who've been here since the dawn of time are still a fucking mystery. Literally half the population is involved in a damn mystery that no one is racing to solve.

For now, I'm still in it. My therapist and doctor have a plan to help me. In addition to the talk therapy, we started addressing some of the other symptoms holistically, like insomnia, for one. A lack of sleep can spin you out, so I take a little cocktail of things like CBD oil, melatonin, and vitamins, and that has worked wonders. When my period came back, I had every crazy craving for gluten, alcohol, and dairy—all the things that make you feel better emotionally—but they actually exacerbated the symptoms of pain and bleeding. So now I am more careful about that. I no longer have the passive suicidal ideation, but if I ever do again, I will be able to recognize it and take steps to get in front of it.

I began the work of separating symptoms from who I really am. Dwyane and I started speaking again, but it took six days, and was probably helped by my increase in talk therapy. And, there is another great voice in my life that has helped me. Not my instinct, but my beloved Brené Brown podcast. It was while I listened to her explain how to give a great apology and how to receive one that I realized what was really wrong. I heard that voice of instinct make a murmur of recognition of a truth: I didn't need to die—what I needed was a simple, heartfelt apology. I seized on the clarity, and asked for one from Dwyane that I received with grace.

See? Only when we identify the issue do we have any hope of really treating it. That's real wisdom.

If you need someone to talk to:
National Suicide Prevention Lifeline, 1-800-273-TALK (8255)

19

DON'T WORRY, MOMMY

I step back out into our yard just as Kaavia James is about to go down her slide. It's my daughter's favorite part of the house play set we painted to match our home. Kaav's halfway down when she looks past Dwyane to catch sight of me. The second her feet hit the ground, she races toward me. Her arms are spread as wide as a two-and-a-half-year-old's can get, ready to wrap around me. My legs, my body if I bend to her—whatever she can get, she is coming for.

I should note that I went inside the house for *two minutes* to get my water.

"Mommy, Mommy!" she says, as if she can't believe the luck that we both happen to be here in this moment. Like, "What are *you* doing here?"

"Kaavia James," I answer, kneeling and smiling to receive the freight train of a hug. She is in a Mommy stage. And you know what? I love it. When she first started doing it, I worried that even my own kid could tell I was stressed and was trying to cheer me up. She got an email from corporate that said, "Hey, we're looking at the productivity numbers and this week we'd really like you to try to say 'Mommy' a lot. Just bring her in more, make her part of the team."

But it's unmistakably genuine and I am reveling in it. She splashes joy around and lets it fall everywhere with a sureness that there will be more. You *want* a Kaav hug. There is nothing like her looking upon you, sizing up the essence of you, and still giving you that "whup, bring it in" embrace. You feel like you just landed a tentpole movie.

"Mommy. Mommy? Mommy." She says my name again and again, a different inflection each time, trying to get my attention when she already has all of it. I repeat her name back to her to show I'm listening to whatever it is she has to say, but give up and simply let her lead me by the hand. "Mommy," she says one last time, this one low and to herself.

Kaavia James takes me to where she has sat her dolls to watch her play in her house. There are four of them, all perfectly placed in a lawn chair she has dragged over just for them. She looks around for a second for another chair for me, then tugs my hand downward as she points to the ground.

I dutifully sit, and she places her hand to my face and smiles. "Don't worry, Mommy."

"Okay," I reply. "I won't worry."

"Don't worry, Mommy," is her phrase for any perceived road-block. Not only me doing without a chair, which is fine, but her refusal to share a cookie, which is maybe not as fine. Or me breaking it to her that we cannot build a snowman when there is no snow.

As quick as she assures me, she takes off again for her play set, and turns back only to check on the dolls next to me. All four have to go everywhere with her, always in her line of sight. There is Baby—a little Black baby doll with hard plastic hair—and Chimmy, a yellow-hoodied puppy inspired by Jimin from the K-pop band BTS. Core to the group are Seal-ie 1 and Seal-ie 2, two lavender aromatherapy stuffed seals, tan and white with black whiskers.

The four dolls can never be separated, but even in a group hug or sitting, the Seal-ies have to be tight together. We used to switch them out as one got dirty, but since she realized there are two, they always have to be together. I take this bond seriously, and I always think of *The Color Purple*'s Celie and her sister Nettie. "Nothing but death can keep me from her," Nettie screams as Mister tries to tear them apart forever. Under Kaav's watch, these Seal-ies shall never be parted.

When we go anywhere in the car, she locks all four together in a seat belt. When she eats, they watch her. If she is swimming in our pool and a Santa Ana wind breezes through to knock one off their perch watching her, she gets out of the pool to right them so they don't miss a stroke.

"Watch," Kaavia James yells to them now as she climbs the rock wall of her little house, and I instinctively turn to them to make sure they are.

I was not a girl who played with dolls. When I first started getting toys for Kaavia James I steered away from dolls and "stuffies," as I found out grown-ass people had taken to calling stuffed animals. I didn't see the fun in them, so what was their use? They sneaked in as gifts, and she seized upon them. It turns out this girl who has everything loves most of all to play Mommy. Mostly she reenacts her own nighttime routine, and is constantly getting her four dolls ready for bed. You've never seen babies nap as much as these do. Constantly being woken only to be put back to sleep.

"Shh, shh, shh," she says, a finger to her mouth before a whisper of "Baby sleeping." Kaav's baby area is right next to where she plays Food Truck, which is a burger and taco stand play set. She'll work while they sleep, and I feel a tinge of pride as I narrate her life. "She's an entrepreneur! She's a mom! She *can* have it all."

When Kaavia James began focusing on me in this Mommy stage she's in, I actually wondered if it was because time with me had become a precious resource as I worked more. Mommy disappeared to go into her office or to a set, my version of working the Food Truck. It occurs to me now that I was looking for a reason for my daughter to love me, and had settled on a *lack* of me as the reason. What if she just loved me because I was? Who I am, where I am.

Dwyane comes to sit next to me on the ground, putting his hands back on the grass. He talks about a flight he has to take to Atlanta tomorrow, but truthfully, I am only half listening because I am watching Kaav race around. I marvel again at how fast she is, and I see Dwyane's exact running style, superhuman fast but with the slight pigeon-toe gait that some of the world's best athletes have. My husband and Kaavia James hold their mouths the same way, their brows knit the same in concentration. How many times have I taken a picture of the same expression on each face, determined to capture the perfect side-by-side?

Like a shot, she is beside us again, but goes to her dolls first. "Chimmy," she says lightly, grabbing the puppy in a hug sweetly. Then, as she puts him back, her voice drops to the low bass of a fraternity brother greeting a beloved friend at a bar. *"Chimmy."* This is one of the funny voices she has picked up from me in my unending quest to make her laugh.

Because I will do anything to hear that laugh. In the same way that she says my name again and again to assure herself I really am right there—who I am, where I am—I need to hear that laugh over and over because it is my purest feeling of happiness. In my life, joy was something that was always snatched from me, so I never wanted to be caught looking for it. If it came, it came. And don't hold it too close, 'cause if you show something is valuable to you, it will be snatched away.

But Kaav's laugh fills every moment, every "now," with abundance. Why be miserly or fearful about joy when we have so much here in this second? It is here now—use it, study it, hug it close, or hand it to someone you love, but do something with this moment, because you have it. We have it. The immediacy of a two-year-old's needs and joys—the perpetual present tense of childhood—will remind you that *this* is the moment that matters.

Kaav turns quickly from her dolls and leaps at Dwyane and me. She puts her two arms around our necks, almost knocking our heads together *Three Stooges* style. She falls on top of us, as only a two-year-old can, knowing the people who love her the most will be a soft, if groaning and creaking, place to land.

"Oof," I say, flat on my back, looking up at the blue, cloudless sky above us. She laughs, and we laugh with her as she hugs my body like a pillow to rest on.

"Don't worry, Mommy," she says.

"I won't worry," I promise, meaning it in this perfect now.

20

STANDARDS AND PRACTICES

A TRAGEDY IN THREE ACTS

During the slave regime, the Southern white man owned the Negro body and soul. It was to his interest to dwarf the soul and preserve the body.

—Ida B. Wells, *The Red Record*, 1895

Last summer, when Ida B. Wells won a posthumous Pulitzer for her investigative reporting, I sat down to read *Southern Terrors* and *The Red Record*. Respectively, they are her 1892 and 1895 accounts of the racial terrorism of the lynching of Black people in the three decades after Emancipation. I had read excerpts of Wells in college, but never the full texts. I downloaded them on my phone and was again struck by her detailing of the massacre of Black men and women in the South, often successful businesspeople who competed with white neighbors, and the desecration of their bodies in death. Ida B. Wells pointed out that the murder of Black people could be indiscriminate after Emancipation because they were no longer property. Black bodies belonged to nobody but themselves, so harming them was no injury to another white man. However, it was still in the interest of oppressors to dwarf Black souls through systematic terrorism.

The torture Wells described was beyond horrific, and she could recount these murders so well because white publications reported every grisly detail to serve as a warning and taunt to Black people. The vivid prose of violent death, the more lurid the better, could reach an even wider audience than the one witnessing the Black body left desecrated in a town square. The detail was not a taunt of "Look what we did," but a louder, sterner warning to all Black people: "Look what we can do to you."

So, we know of Richard Neal. On February 11, 1893, Mr. Neal became the fourth documented Black person lynched in Shelby County, Tennessee, within a fifteen-month period. Wells quotes the *Memphis Scimitar,* which detailed Mr. Neal being brought for identification to Mrs. Jack White, who said she was raped and was *almost* certain he was the man. "If he isn't the man, he is exactly like him."

The newspaper recounts Mr. Neal being lynched by two hundred people, "the best people" of the surrounding neighborhoods, who acted "without passion or exhibition of anger." These details are not striking to any Black person today, who knows that our existence is probable cause for violence and that whatever results, there will be "fine people on both sides."

But it was this sentence from the *Memphis Scimitar* that stopped me: "The body was perfectly limber when the Sheriff's posse cut it down and retained enough heat to warm the feet of Deputy Perkins, whose road cart was converted into a hearse."

I sat with that, and it stays with me. A dead Black man used for heat. That warmth, and the soul that inhabited that Black body, had no value until it could be used by Deputy Perkins for comfort. And isn't that the story we're still told? Anything Black—an idea, a rhythm, a style, our souls—can be put to better use by a white person.

A feeling of danger crept up on me as Ida B. Wells connected the dots in the 125 years between us. The souls of Black folk are still being dwarfed and snuffed out, and our bodies still ravaged for our parts. To get laughs or get ahead, white people try on our skin, our curves, our voices . . . anything is up for grabs. They take the things Black children are taught to hate and change about themselves: our color, our hair, our ass, our speech, our experience. We're supposed to get rid of all that. We are encouraged to adopt whatever is equated with whiteness, exchanging our features, language, or value system.

And while we throw away the things that make us Black, white people are waiting in the wings with catcher's mitts. Ready to take whatever we cast off.

These parts, like the body of Mr. Neal, are then freely used, whether that takes the form of persistent use of blackface, or through blackfishing, the appropriation of our culture and physical features to access wealth and opportunities. Meanwhile, we are slaughtered—in our streets, our cars, our homes—and our bleeding, asphyxiated bodies are recorded and packaged into quickly consumed trauma bites of entertainment that we cannot escape. Modern versions of the newspaper articles that Wells compiled to reveal as scare-tactic taunting of Black people.

To confuse us, these practices are disguised as serving the interests of Black people. Modern blackface, we're told, is used as a "critique" of racist tropes, blackfishing is a "celebration" of our features, and the video loop of brutalized Black bodies is "information" used to stir the conscience of white people. If you feel some type of way about it—if these three things actually feel like dehumanization, exploitation, and defilement—then you're too sensitive.

So, the violence continues. *State the facts,* I hear Ida B. Wells say across the years between us. "The way to right wrongs is to turn the light of truth upon them."

Lights, please. Let the show begin.

ACT ONE: BLACKFACE

On the benefits of playing at—and with—
Blackness, unless of course you're Black

I had no idea cuss words were so important before I started producing TV. As an actress, I was aware of the last-minute script changes that came down from a network's Standards and Practices department. But it was only when I was more involved in the creation of those scripts that I understood the horse-trading of curses and storylines involved in enforcing FCC regulations protecting the eyes and ears of American audiences.

"Well, they'll give us two 'shits,'" a showrunner on *Being Mary Jane* would say, "but we have to cut the 'fuck' if it's meant in a sexual way." My character could say it if she burned her finger baking, but not if she was expressing desire. I vaguely remember that we had an unlimited number of "bitches" to use.

I respected these decisions, or at least understood that the people in Standards and Practices feared FCC fines. Like what happened to the PBS affiliate that did an afternoon airing of Martin Scorsese's documentary film series *The Blues,* in which one too many Black musicians swore one too many times. If they came after PBS, what hope did BET have? Best to play it safe, and cut anything that might offend.

I thought back to all the hoops we went through for Standards and Practices on Blackface Amnesty Day. That's not what it was actually called, but in the summer of 2020, during the Black Lives Matter protests against systemic racism, an urgent call went out among network execs and creatives to destroy evidence of the use of blackface in their shows. The racism was quickly removed from streaming and on-demand services. These shows that used blackface were not *Amos 'n' Andy* reruns with Kingfish working a scheme in black and white. Blackface or brownface was used on five episodes of *It's Always Sunny in Philadelphia,* four *30 Rock*s, three *Scrubs,* and single episodes of *The Office, Mad Men,* and *Community,* among others. All of these streaming cash cows carried the accolades of television's finest offerings. The list of popular sitcoms and dramas undergoing edit and deletion was so long that news sites ran lists of specific episodes leaving streaming and syndication: Like Pokémon for racism, "gotta catch 'em all."

I have to ask, *Standards and Practices gave me two "shits," but never gave* one *about the racism of blackface?* They had a scientific formula to how much of a butt cheek you should show, but there was no consideration of harm whatsoever for people shellacking their faces and putting on Afros to make a visual joke of my features. Because these instances of blackface didn't just happen. TV takes a lot. You first have to have the blackface idea, bring it to the writers' room, put it to paper, get the makeup, wigs, and prosthetics, light the different skin tone, perform the racist bit, get the blessing of Standards and Practices, edit it, and send it out. There was no one empowered, at any of those steps, to say, "That's racist"? No one noticed?

As these episodes were deleted, creators dashed off sentences of "we know better now." But most of the blackface mentioned was shown at least a full two years after a February 2006 interview in which Dave Chappelle—the most influential comedian of that era—went on *The Oprah Winfrey Show* and called blackface "the visual personification of the n-word." I want to assure you that blackface has been offensive since its creation, something that has been said repeatedly by Black people. There's not one of us who has ever said, "You know what'd be fun here? Some blackface." But these white creators also knew it was offensive, and I point to the Chappelle moment as a marker of time: what he said could not escape the notice of *anyone* working in comedy or TV production after 2006. Still, *30 Rock* relied heavily on blackface, using it in 2008, twice in 2010, and again in 2012.

As these episodes were disappeared, creators either offered no comment or crafted tortured sentences apologizing for the pain these images caused. I am struck that these "images" and "tropes" are apparently walking and talking, bursting into writers' rooms to wreak havoc with their violence. "I'm sorry you were hurt," says the creator standing above you with the machete. "It was this darned knife." The apology is only for the pain the jokes have caused, blaming the knife for the murder.

Because this is not just about hurt feelings. Blackface goes beyond humiliation to the point of violence. To not understand the insidious nature of racism as violence is to not understand that you have fucked Black people over for years. There should be a real consequence, in the same way that we have suffered real consequences from your shit.

The intention, we are told, is humor. But what the fuck was so funny? I have to ask: In that moment, what were they laughing at? Even if the joke is the absurdity of this person doing that? And who, exactly, is tickled by the violence of blackface? I would really like to know. If I walked around that set with my Black-ass skin, I wouldn't think it was funny. No, the few Black people who make it into those creative spaces go home and say to their loved ones, "Today they thought Blackness was a joke."

Because those white spaces, these shows with predominantly white execs, white stars, and white writers, still have Black people on the outskirts. I am thinking in particular of the scenes from a series that occasionally broadcast live, because I have been in that shooting space. I have been the one Black "talent" on the set of places just like that, when the only people I saw who looked like me were a guy at the loading dock or a cleaner. In one of the scenes, an actor does an *Amos 'n' Andy* homage, appearing from a door to say "Here I is, Alfie," in exaggerated blackface with an Afro and dirty overalls. Just on sight the audience went *wild* in an explosion of laughter. On another live episode, the same actor plays a person with a hand transplant, the hand coming from a recently executed Black prisoner. The joke is that the Black hand has a mind of its own, reaching up to strangle him. They demonized and criminalized the hand, and furthered the stereotype that all Black people are plotting to kill whitey—even when their body parts are separated from their souls. It's in their nature, you see. What has struck me is that was the East Coast broadcast, and maybe they lost their nerve about showing racism to the West Coast, since the joke is that it's now a white woman's hand, one that sexually assaults him.

Between scenes, when the actor walked around in blackface, did he see a young Black worker on set? Did he maybe blush under his shoe polish, and stop to explain to her why it was funny? How it was part of a bit, and she had to understand this was not *him*? Yes, they were two human beings who happened to be sharing space for a moment when one was humiliating and dehumanizing the other, but it wasn't *real*. She shouldn't believe her eyes, she had to trust him. Did the writer come over to them, to vouch for the actor and the script and assure her this was funny? Did the producers chime in? Tell the young Black woman that if it caused her pain to see in the moment, then at least that hurt was in service of something greater: a bit?

Because the bit had an intention, right? When I talked this out with people who hadn't seen the blackface, one woman said, "Well, what was the intention? Intention is important." So, what *was* the intention? When shows repeatedly do blackface, what are the creators saying? And what is the intention when Standards and Practices does not find racism harmful to the audience?

These are smart people who know that blackface is rooted in oppression and pain. They cannot plead an ignorance of the context that this strips us of humanity. So yes, they want us to know something by repeatedly mining our pain for laughs, but they don't actually want to have that conversation. I ask them: What is it that you want us to know but are afraid to say to our faces? Because you feel like we might punch you in *your* face? You want us to feel less than? Perhaps we've made too much noise about being oppressed. You want us to always feel maligned and made a joke of? Or is it that you want us to be harmed?

Because this is what I see: White folks putting on grotesque versions of my skin. My hair. What they perceive to be my mannerisms. They want to take their pick of my Black features and put them to work in the service of their jokes.

Let's call them what they are: nigger jokes. They're not stupid enough to tell a nigger joke in the presence of Black people, because there will be consequences. But they can tell nigger jokes in the cultivated *absence* of Black power. That's what lets them get away with it.

I can hear people defensively saying that comedy is about pushing boundaries. *This* particular performance is a satiric critique of black-face for the "benefit" of Black people. The intent is satire, you see. The irony is these people think they are taking on the mantle of Richard Pryor, furthering the boundaries of what is possible in comedy. But to be transgressive is to move *beyond* a boundary. They are in fact being *regressive,* shoring up old institutions of racism in comedy, revitalizing the tried-and-true formula of minstrelsy.

Beginning in the 1830s, white actors toured America in wildly popular shows with their faces smeared in black cork, dressed in rags to play cruel stereotypes like Zip Coon, Old Darkie, Mammy, and Dandy, the one who put on airs like a white man, acting as if he was "a real person." It's why "Jim Crow"—the good-for-nothing fool that was such a stock character on the circuit—came to be shorthand for the post-emancipation segregation laws that codified the disciplinary power of white supremacy. These traveling shows weren't just successful in forging dehumanizing stereotypes into archetypes that still fuel racial bias today; they made a tremendous amount of money and formed the foundation of America's entertainment industry— the industry these contemporary white performers of blackface and I still share. Show business has had this song-and-dance fantasy of white superiority going on forever.

The twenty-first-century iteration of blackface has the knowing nod of "Do you believe we're getting away with this?" But that's just keeping up with trends. Minstrel acts have always morphed to reflect the time and medium. The only reason minstrel shows stopped was now you could see blackface at the movies. The year 1914 gave us the early short film *Coon Town Suffragettes,* which managed to be on trend mocking both Black people and women seeking the vote. One hundred years later, on *It's Always Sunny in Philadelphia*, the actress Kaitlin Olson did blackface with her actor husband, Rob McElhenney, who is also the creator and executive producer of the show. The excuse for the actors to do blackface is that the characters are doing a *Lethal Weapon* parody, with McElhenney playing Danny Glover's role. On the set, while Olson went for a coal-black shoe-polish blackface with mammy red lips, McElhenney went for his version of "authenticity," going to Autonomous FX, a prosthetic and makeup studio specializing in horror and animal effects, to have his blackface done. They provided a silicone nose—broad and flat for comedic punch—and a silicone forehead to better accent a short Afro wig.

Olson was so proud of the blackface that she brought what she thought was a hilarious story about it to the couch at *Conan* in 2013. She and her husband were filming in blackface on location when she cut her leg. "Then we went to the emergency room and everyone's staring at us," she told Conan O'Brien. "After a while I realized they're not staring out of concern, they're like glaring at us. Finally, I looked at Rob and I was like, 'Why are they . . . oh, right.'" The audience at home then saw the reveal of a shot of McElhenney in blackface. Conan's studio audience roared with approving laughter. Olson continued, knowing they had nailed the visual joke of Blackness. "It was the blackface that they were glaring at. Then it made sense."

Olson and McElhenney were still very proud of their blackface when they both returned to *Conan* in 2015 with the rest of the all-white cast, including Danny DeVito, Charlie Day, and Glenn Howerton. To continue the "joke" away from the context of the show and in real life, they pointedly acted as if nothing was amiss when

Conan showed another photo of them in blackface and asked if they received "any blowback."

"No, we were playing Black people," said McElhenney, as if he didn't get why this would be an issue.

"How could you play Black people without getting fully black?" answered Olson. "We didn't just do the face, we did the whole body."

In the face of this willful indifference for laughs, Danny DeVito offered to McElhenney, "By the way, she's a lot darker than you. Look at that shot. She's like really *Black*. You look like a Mexican."

More laughter.

Their costar Charlie Day immediately jumped in. "The thing is, blackface, that's like a generality," he said. "That's specific Danny Glover face, so you're really only insulting one person." The cast agreed the only person who had the right to be upset would be Danny Glover, and Glenn Howerton—also a writer and executive producer on the show—joked that Glover had called to ask why they didn't just hire him. "I could use the work."

Why involve him and risk a consequence for your actions, when you can just take what you need?

There is no upside to speaking up in a significant way about this. People like them will say I am not edgy. Not humorous. Not a team player. I am tying the hands of creatives. After all, Black comedians have made many jokes about Blackness and oppression and all the things that make up the collective Black experience. But they can do that without negating any of it, because these are jokes that are mined from their own lives. If it's not their lived experience, they are simply interlopers. Their sole intention has been to do harm.

Besides not appearing to be a team player, there is this reason not to speak up: Black people know that to do so is to enter a devil's bargain. It is not just opening ourselves up to the PTSD that comes from sharing personal pain. That might be enough to silence people. No, it's that we, the victims, will be portrayed as the assailants.

Let me lead the uninitiated through it. Take a straightforward situation—you overhear a coworker calling you a racial slur, or, say, a celebrity producer repeatedly uses blackface on their show. In law, this can be called an intentional infliction of emotional distress—the tort of outrage. The defendant acted intentionally or even recklessly, and the victimized party is due damages for the emotional distress. Even if you, the victim, aren't awarded monetary damages, some justice is expected, right? Your racist coworker can be fired, for example. The blackface perpetrators should at least lose some standing in polite society. Open and shut.

Wrong. Almost immediately, the clear case is muddied by obscuring intent. Namely, they either didn't mean to be racist or you took it the wrong way. Fine, we have all seen that happen. It's the aforementioned "this knife did it, not me" defense strategy. Comedians don't hurt people, jokes do.

When that doesn't immediately work, the next step is making the racist perpetrator just as much a victim as you. This isn't just the sudden white-girl tears that can make any request for accountability seem like an assault. No, this is a proven plan of action that happens formally in HR offices and in the newsrooms that set public opinion. In this plan, the racist apologizes—sometimes in a letter, sometimes thirdhand, but there's some statement—and you are asked to accept that and move on. You are reminded of the stakes: the racist's livelihood and reputation are at risk. Are you going to take that from them? After all, the perpetrator has lowered himself to reason with *you*. Can you imagine how humiliating this must be to beg *you* for mercy? Hasn't the racist suffered enough?

Boom, we now have two victims. If you press on, ask for real accountability, you are now the bully. You find yourself asking the same question as the people who want you to be reasonable: *Why did you even say anything?*

So, by speaking up about the harm of blackface, I am the bully. If I name names, it's me who'll hang. But there is one thing they forget. A cover-up can prove intent. I have been on enough cop shows to know that when someone hides the evidence, it's because they know they are guilty of a crime and are afraid of the consequences. In fact, we are told these shows that used blackface define a golden age of television, one that will be studied by culture critics for decades to come. But if a historian who did not witness the racism they employed wants to study race in twenty-first-century America, or even convey a wholly accurate description of what these shows broadcast as popular culture, they cannot.

Who does that serve? Certainly not some comedy-loving kid who wants to study the era and looks like me. They deserve the truth. My grandchildren won't have a full picture of the life I lived and worked in. "Gramma talked about some fuckshit," they'll say in a phrase that Standards and Practices would flag. "But I can't find it."

The grandchildren of these blackface artists won't learn from their sins, either. They will be free, like so many people today, to enjoy their generational wealth without concern that it came at anyone's expense. The crime simply never happened. The legacies of these shows will remain intact, the hands of their creators whitewashed clean.

ACT TWO: BLACKFISHING

When there is nothing about Blackness—on a
Black person—that is our own to keep

I follow a lot of Black women on Instagram, you know, being a Black woman and all. So, whenever I do a search, my Instagram's Explore page is always offering up "discoveries" from accounts the algorithm thinks I should encounter. This morning the main page was a young white woman taking a pouty full-length side shot in the mirror. Her hair was in two thick braids, which fell down the back she had arched to accentuate the lift of her butt in Adidas sportswear. Her makeup was contoured to reshape her face, and she was wearing a foundation or bronzer that was several shades darker than her white hand.

"Issa vibe," was her caption.

This was blackfishing, caught white-handed. There is a crime wave of non-Black people—mainly women—stealing the looks and features of Blackness for profit. While I know they do this to get ahead, I am so conditioned by growing up in this society that it is hard to comprehend how approximating Blackness could help anyone. From birth, Black women are told to change. When my daughter Kaavia James was just days old, I caught more than one person peeling back the baby mittens she wore to keep herself from scratching her eyes or skin. They needed to see her nail beds, because that would reveal what Blackness she would have to face. Understand, colorism from within the Black community springs from terrorism by the white community.

They terrorize us into looking and acting like them. We will not be hired. We will not be chosen for love. We will not be believed when we are harmed. We will be stopped on the street and in cars by police. Our lives will be daily terror, but we can help ourselves, we are told, if we just move toward whiteness. Cut our noses, straighten our hair, stay out of the sun to not get even darker, lose our asses, starve ourselves to fit a shape that is unnatural to us. Shed our language and culture unless it can be used as currency in transaction with the white community. Leave our Blackness. Treat Blackness like a beauty queen who has to leave her small town for the better life she is meant to have.

And to the victor go the spoils of what's been abandoned. They mine it for humor, for art and music, and then when that is exhausted, they pillage our body parts and mannerisms once they realize those things can offer advantages. Curves, hair, skin tones, a "blaccent," style . . . soon they are co-opting our whole-ass selves. These body parts and mannerisms were no good to the Black people who were taught to reject them. But if you're white, the embrace makes you edgy, cool, and attractive. Soon they are taking our pain and oppression, "identifying with it," and turning it into a currency that's only worth something when it's taken from us.

Plenty of people are profiting from stealing our looks, but when we talk about blackfishing, the media goes to what they see as the extreme cases of those who have assumed *entire* Black identities over the last few years. There is Rachel Dolezal, who posed as a Black woman to secure a platform as head of her local NAACP chapter and then got a book deal; Jennifer Krug, a white woman from Kansas, who fabricated a story of being a Black girl from the Bronx conceived from rape so she could become a tenured professor at a private university; and Jennifer Benton, who became—I am not making this up—Satchuel Paigelyn Cole to steal a platform in the Indianapolis social justice movement.

These women are extreme cases of the much more pervasive

movement of blackfishing, where parts and portions of us are tried on for use. But they point to a larger issue: the reason that blackfishing is so prevalent and profitable is because of the prioritization of lighter-skinned Black women. This is true interracially, and, as Black women will tell you—and a lot of Black men will admit as fact—intraracially. There would not be such a space for blackfishing if lightness were not so prized in our community. Lighter-skinned women are seen not just as stereotypical status symbols in relationships, but as cleaner, more feminine, and more intelligent. Meanwhile, Black women whose lives and physical characteristics are rooted in their Blackness are always the last option. I have been told repeatedly that one of the reasons Black women celebrate my marriage is that Dwyane did not choose to marry a light-skinned woman when his wealth and fame gave him access to them. That is some shit.

Those three charlatans—Dolezal, Krug, and Benton—were readily embraced by white and Black people as professors and activists because as light-skinned women (even fake) they were seen as a bridge to whiteness. It's interesting to examine the Black folks that white people run to. They might be biracial or married to white people, but in some larger way, their lives center whiteness, the white gaze, and white acceptance.

I am thinking of two women who have found each other on the edge of my circle, a white woman who co-opts Blackness, taking the language and the cause, but leaving the oppression to others to deal with, and a Black woman she is in business with, who has told me that race is a state of identity similar to being transgender. Leaving aside how wrong that is about the trans identity—the idea that their identity is something to put on or take off at will—it revealed to me how that friendship and business relationship works. They are each issuing each other a pass to visit their respective worlds. "I will grant you access to Blackness and allow you to feel comfortable co-opting it, and in return, I will benefit from your privilege." There is a give and take, but in this transaction, it is the white woman whose needs are centered.

I have white friends. I say this to be funny, because that's what racists always say, right? "I can't be racist, I have a Black friend." Have they been to that Black person's home? Are they in a picture in that Black person's home, or is this a transactional working relationship? If they feel that close, they should go ask their Black friend if they're racist then. But I really do have white friends in my close circle, and they are that close because they do not use the intimacy of friendship as an opportunity for co-opting my identity. They allow themselves to try to understand the complexity and richness of Blackness, something I, and they, could spend a lifetime doing.

And maybe that is what adds the insult to the violence of blackface and blackfishing. When an actor or actress does blackface, they choose the black shoe polish of dress shoes, because to be the Blackest of Black people is the joke. When women do blackfishing, it's not the richness and diversity within blackness that they so covet, it's the feeling of being exoticized and prioritized.

Whether mined for jokes or access, we're all just things in a pile to be grabbed. Black, with no difference from one to the next. And the bodies are piling up.

ACT THREE: BLACK BODIES ON AUTOPLAY

The enduring entertainment of lynching

"If it bleeds, it leads," goes the adage of getting news watchers hooked, and I would add that if it's Black and bleeds, you can repeat that violence over and over without care. I don't use "it" by accident. More and more, Black bodies are becoming commodities, disposable stars for a news cycle. It is ironic that these creators of scripted television only rushed to remove their offensive content in the summer of 2020, when American eyes were glued to the nine minutes and twenty-nine seconds that Officer Derek Chauvin knelt on the neck of George Floyd until he was dead on the ground in Minneapolis. The same screens that show us as figures of fun and laughter will, in one short social media scroll, show our bodies brutalized and snuffed out in shaky videos from cell phones and police body cams.

There are countless videos available for repeat viewing of Black people, young and old, being abused or murdered by police or people who feel they are in authority. Besides Mr. Floyd, there are videos of the shootings, beatings, abuse, and choke-hold strangulations of Eric Garner in Staten Island; Tamir Rice in Cleveland; Oscar Grant in Oakland; Laquan McDonald, Ronald Johnson, Harith Augustus, and Jemel Roberson in separate Chicago incidents; Dajerria Becton in McKinney, Texas; Stephon Clark in Sacramento; Sandra Bland in Prairie View, Texas; Walter Scott in North Charleston, South Carolina; Rose Campbell in Alpharetta, Georgia; Decynthia Clements in Elgin, Illinois; Alton Sterling in Baton Rouge; Philando Castile in Falcon Heights, Minnesota; Jhasmynn Sheppard in Tuscaloosa, Alabama; Dyma Loving in Miami-Dade County; Trayford Pellerin in Lafayette, Louisiana; Ahmaud Arbery in Glynn County, Georgia; Geraldine Townsend in Bartlesville, Oklahoma; Anthony McClain in Pasadena; Jazmine Headley in Brooklyn; Stephanie Bottom in Salisbury, North Carolina; Maurice Gordon on New Jersey's Garden State Parkway; Elijah McClain in Aurora, Colorado; Tye Anders and his ninety-year-old grandmother on their front lawn in Midland, Texas; Jacob Blake in Kenosha, Wisconsin; Atatiana Jefferson, shot and killed through the bedroom window of her Fort Worth home, where she was playing video games with her eight-year-old nephew Zion; Izell Richardson, Jr. in Port Allen, Louisiana; Michael Brown in Ferguson, Missouri; Rayshard Brooks in Atlanta; Tony McDade in Tallahassee, Florida; Sterling Brown in Milwaukee; Nika Nicole Holbert in Nashville; Dijon Kizzee in Los Angeles; Deon Kay in Washington, D.C.; Daniel Prude in Rochester, New York; Lymond Moses in New Castle, Delaware; David Tovar Jr. in San Jose, California; Walter Wallace Jr. in Philadelphia; Caron Nazario in Windsor, Virginia; Lyndani Myeni in Honolulu; Daunte Wright in Brooklyn Center, Minnesota; Ma'Khia Bryant in Columbus, Ohio . . .

This is not even a complete list from a new genre of snuff films, Black pain monetized as content to be consumed. News outlets almost apologize if there is not a supply of video of a killing or beating, and in those cases they compensate with descriptions of these horrific murders again and again. Or they show "final moments caught on film"—surveillance footage of the minutes leading up to the "deadly stop" or "police incident." The person is at a convenience store or walking home, the kind of normal, everyday things that the victims of the lynchings Ida B. Wells covered might have been doing when they were made an example of.

As news outlets and social media users attract viewers and clicks with the promise of death—and local news stations run YouTube ads with the clips—I have to ask: Is this for information? Or titillation? They are obviously showing people our pain because they don't think viewers will turn away. There is an undeniable consumer base to watch our deaths. Take the video of Jacob Blake, the twenty-nine-year-old father of six who was shot in the back seven times on August 23, 2020, in Kenosha, Wisconsin. The initial cell phone video went viral, but his attempted murder was packaged and repackaged again and again as news. I've watched so many "versions" of Mr. Blake's story, and took note of the individual slants of news agencies.

And then I noticed something, first in a *CBS This Morning* package on the shooting. Someone in the comments posted a time stamp of the exact moment shots are fired into Mr. Blake's back. I noticed this in another video, this one of Deon Kay, newly nineteen years old, in Washington, D.C.

"Can someone give me the time stamp?" a viewer asked in a comment. Another death watcher quickly gave him the exact moment young Mr. Kay is shot in the chest and begins to bleed out.

Get to the moment that matters. Get to the money shot of our death. The distribution of our pain is clickbait. Attention must be paid to our murders, but without real accountability the murder loop will just continue, one death indistinguishable from another.

Did I used to think that if people saw how we were treated in the streets, there would be some recognition of our humanity? Yes, I did. I retweeted these images of our pain and death with the hope that I would reach somebody who didn't get it. Even though I knew better, I kept the door open for just a sliver of hope for people to give a shit about us. It never felt worth it in the end, but it was that hope that made me do it. Maybe *this* murder, even though there have been countless murders on a loop. But maybe this one, given *this* set of circumstances . . .

I don't have that impulse any more. There will always be an excuse for the brutalization of our bodies. Always. It is what Ida B. Wells witnessed: that lynching—and the past's version of going viral with details in newspapers—was how segregation standards and practices were enforced once Black people were "free." Police-led violence and the unending loop of murder footage are just the modern spin. For all the talk of how cell phones have transformed civil rights, there are very few cases where a cop caught on camera is convicted of murder or assault. Perhaps they are indicted, but by the time they get off, there have likely been six new murders. Even on April 21, 2021, when a jury delivered a just verdict—not to be confused with justice—against Minneapolis police officer Derek Chauvin for the murder of George Floyd, within *minutes* news sites advertised the promise of a new video. This one was of a Columbus, Ohio, police officer firing four shots at sixteen-year-old Ma'Khia Bryant to kill her.

There's about as much justice delivered as there was when Wells covered the ways Black death was turned into entertainment. In her time, people gathered for highly produced, broad-daylight events with the kids in tow. It was the big show. Wells describes parents holding children up high so they could get a better look. Now kids just have YouTube.

Still, Black people are told that allowing people to watch our bodies being desecrated on repeat serves some higher purpose of enlightenment. The enlightenment of white people, that is, because Black people certainly don't need to be convinced of our humanity. But the pulling of heartstrings with an arresting visual has worked before, right? We are told the fable that white northerners were "moved to action" in the summer of 1963 when they turned on the news to see footage of Bull Connor's dogs rending the flesh of Black children. It was part of King's plan, we are told, to prick the sleepy consciences of white America.

That was the audience that mattered. Not the Black viewers, who felt rage not just at what they saw on-screen but in their lives. People in the North also faced constant public harassment and the strangled opportunities of employment, housing, and education. It was the lived experiences of Black people that led to uprisings all over America, not just the Deep South. Los Angeles; Wichita; Nashville; Omaha; Chicago; Cincinnati; Cleveland; Louisville; Minneapolis; Newark; Harlem; Detroit; Washington, D.C.; Cambridge, Maryland; Rochester, New York; Chester, Pennsylvania . . . That rage didn't come from what they saw on-screen in a faraway place, but in their daily lives. There is no place, east, west, north, or south that is free of anti-Blackness and a propping up of white supremacy. That magical land does not exist.

That's not the narrative we are fed. The story we are told starts on May 3, 1963, in Birmingham, Alabama, when a photographer caught a shot of a German shepherd lunging to bite what is captioned usually as "a young Black boy," and rarely is the "B" capitalized. He is actually Walter Gadsden, then a tenth grader, but for history's purposes he is just a Black boy.

The photo of young Mr. Gadsden's assault appeared in the *New York Times* the next day, getting the attention of President John F. Kennedy. As King put it a week later, "When that picture went all over Asia and Africa and England and France, Mr. Kennedy said, 'Bobby, you better get your assistant down there and look into this matter. It's a dangerous situation for our image abroad.'" King wasn't naïve (and I do appreciate the humor of his saying it would be an assistant sent to Birmingham). Any change would not be about witnessing harm to Black people, but the feared harm to the image of white America. What a network or streaming service today might call a brand.

But what did Walter Gadsden feel when he saw that picture? In 1993, Diane McWhorter contacted Mr. Gadsden for a *Washington Post* article, "The Moment That Made a Movement," about the thirtieth anniversary of the photograph's publication. Throughout the article, McWhorter, the white author of a Pulitzer Prize–winning account of the civil rights movement, *Carry Me Home,* centers the photograph's appeal to white consciences. She does not mention Mr. Gadsden until midway through the article, after she quotes Taylor Branch—another white historian who won a Pulitzer for a civil rights book—talking about what the image meant to "the American mind." When she does say his name, the first thing McWhorter points out is that Walter Gadsden was there because he "had been playing hooky even before the demonstrations made truancy honorable." (McWhorter is kinder to the dogs: "They were already celebrities. The top canine, Rebel, performed before civic groups and school kids all over town.") McWhorter takes pains to downplay the trauma, saying the dogs were only out for "a short half hour," amounting to "a few dog bites."

At the end of the article, McWhorter relates finding the phone number of Gadsden, who at that point, 1993, would have been about my age. "I dialed it," she writes, "anticipating a hometown reunion of sorts." McWhorter was disappointed with his response to reminiscing. "With a cold apprehension, Walter Gadsden told me he did not want to 'become involved' in my story and politely hung up."

I can't know his motives, but I know that at my age you get tired of bullshit. I can guess that he didn't want to become involved in her story about "a few dog bites" because his agency had been removed from the story from the beginning. He was just there, a Black boy. A Black body. Like all the others that would come after him, their names and stories bleeding together until they too are virtually anonymous.

———

"The very frequent inquiry made after my lectures by interested friends is 'What can I do to help the cause?'" Ida B. Wells writes at the end of *The Red Record*. "The answer always is: 'Tell the world the facts.'"

I have questioned the intent of people here who have repeatedly used Blackness for their own ends, so let me be clear that my own intention is to tell the world the facts. I'm offering honest critique to people who should be open to that if they really are about "doing the work" and being change agents. In the same way that I need to be read for filth sometimes if I just refuse to own how my actions might be hurtful.

We need to make people fear doing racist things more than they worry about being held accountable. People have been getting off easy, and this is how 125 years passes and Ida B. Wells's words still ring true. People delete evidence of their racism from TV history so it won't tarnish their legacy and brand. They do a half-ass apology later for the blackfishing post that gets them the reach and impressions to attract sponsors. They run footage of us getting slaughtered and left lying in the street and say it's for our own good. And it all continues.

There is no *Men in Black* moment where we can erase everything that we are subjected to. But there can be real accountability. We can create new standards and practices based on a desire to make amends. We can invite people in power to step aside so that those who do not look like them will be in the space to make decisions. We can stop rewarding people who have proven they don't care about us with passes to do further harm to us.

Yes, caring is exhausting. To be Black, or to be a non-Black person who gives a shit, will wear you the fuck out. But if you really want to be about that life, that's what has to happen.

These are the facts. Tell it to the world.

21

OH, ONE MORE THING

I need a moment with you before we say goodbye.

We have been on the journey of this book together. In a perfect world, this is the time when I would hand you a cliché and call it a map. "Go off and soar!" Or "Dive into vulnerability!" But you and I know better. How can you soar with a broken wing, and your soul barely fed? How can you leap headfirst into being vulnerable when you've had to protect yourself from real harm for years?

It starts within ourselves, with radical self-awareness and truth. Create a space in your mind to process your experiences and ask yourself, *How the fuck did I get here?*

Four years ago, I asked myself that, and I realized that I had been led to where I was by fear. Not just led—fear had motivated, inspired, and controlled my life for decades. Fear is a tool that has its place: it will keep you alive if you are in real danger, but if you live with it day to day it will eventually deaden your soul. Instead of moving from fear, I began, slowly, to extend myself grace, a combination of mercy and love we are deserving of simply because we exist. Because this grace was from me, and for me, I was not dependent on another person for it. It was limitless, and living in that state of grace I have been able to explore vulnerability. I've tried to show that here in this book. Not as a guide for you, but as a companion.

In my mind, I see vulnerability as a body of water. An ocean, a lake, a river, whatever you see, it is yours. I am not saying you have to immediately dive in as soon as you finish this book. We can move slowly along its banks. Test it out and see how it feels. We'll let the waves of transparency wash our skin to cleanse us, until, as we go along, we can dip in a little more.

You can go as slow as you want, but we will be moving forward. When we cut our feet on sharp objects hidden in the muck by the water, we won't hide the pain for fear of being judged. We'll tend to the wound, and refuse to blame our skin for not hardening into numbness.

We are superheroes *because* we bleed. We are great *because* we feel and we tell the truth, and in so doing we create community.

We got this.

ACKNOWLEDGMENTS

I want to thank everyone at Dey Street Books and HarperCollins Publishers for the care they put into this book. Thanks especially to my editor, Carrie Thornton, who has been incredibly supportive of me as a writer from the beginning. I am also indebted to Peter Kispert, Liate Stehlik, Ben Steinberg, Heidi Richter, Kendra Newton, Ploy Siripant, Andrea Molitor, Angela Boutin, Andy LeCount, and Christine Edwards.

Kevin Carr O'Leary, thank you for being the other side of my brain, and for giving me a safe space to lead with all my vulnerabilities—the ones that I thought would be my undoing.

I deeply appreciate my CAA Book Family. Thank you to Cait Hoyt, as well as Kate Childs and Mike Johnston. Thanks also to Chelsea Thomas and Meredith O'Sullivan at the Lede Company. I am grateful to Range Media Partners: David Bugliari, Chelsea McKinnies, and Paige Wandling. I also want to thank Holly Shakoor and Kian Gass.

Thank you to Albert Lee for believing in me. You convinced me my story mattered and should be shared.

I owe so much to Team Wade, who keeps the train on the tracks so D and I can follow my dreams and rest easy knowing our children and everything else are covered: Chantel Cohen, Richard Ingraham, Andrell McCants, Tracy Union, Ronnda Hamilton, Elijah Barreda, Valerie Arguello, Peton Johnson, Mayra Iglesias, Nuris Maritza Gutierrez, Edgar Prado, Nyesha Arrington, Brenda Larson, Xiomara Altamirano, Ayana McKnight, Maria Robles.

The Shenanigans groupchat is a place of sacred trust and profane jokes. Thank you to Essence Atkins, Jason Bolden, Stacey Carter, Chantel Cohen, Daune Cummings, Adair Curtis, Lindsay Faulk, Corinne Kaplan, Kelley Lee, Nicole Lyn, Deirdre Maloney, and Larry Sims.

Thomas Christos, Malika James, Larry Sims, Wankanya Hickson, thank you guys for keeping me sane and fly. Till the wheels fall off.

D, thank you for loving me, supporting me, laughing with me, and going on Twitter rants to have my back.

Thank you to my family for inspiring me to create work that makes them proud.

This book would not be what it is without the trust built by the readers of *We're Going to Need More Wine*. I remember each one of you from the last book tour, the days and nights together that we turned into revivals. I love you, and I am so happy to be with you again.

ABOUT THE AUTHOR

Gabrielle Union is an actress, executive producer, activist, bestselling author, and most recently, a Time100 cover honoree. Union formed her production shingle, I'll Have Another, in 2018 with the goal of telling stories that center marginalized communities with their specific point of views in an authentic manner. In August of 2020, she relaunched her haircare brand, Flawless by Gabrielle Union, for women with textured hair. The new and improved collection includes an array of options, affordably priced between four and ten dollars, that empowers consumers to customize a regimen specific to their texture and style preferences. Prior to relaunching Flawless, Union learned of the disparities in the food space and joined Bitsy's as a cofounder with the goal of making healthy, allergen-friendly, school-safe snacks that are accessible and affordable for all families regardless of their socioeconomic or geographical status. Her first book, *We're Going to Need More Wine: Stories That Are Funny, Complicated and True,* was released in 2017 and instantly became a *New York Times* bestseller. Union serves as a leader and advocate for inclusion in the entertainment industry. She is also a champion of breast health and combating sexual violence.